D1002297

Praise for *Lemon Moms*

This book is terrific. I recommend it to my patients who are working through these kinds of issues.
--Bernard B. Kahan, M.D. Adolescent and Adult Psychiatry

A great deal of support can be taken and shared. *Lemon Moms* is a great starting place to teach the reader how to identify the behaviors, shut down manipulations and remove the drama from their day-to-day interactions with their narcissist, if they are unable to avoid them entirely. Worth reading.
--Victoria Irwin, Editor in Chief, FangirlNation.com

Lemon Moms: A Guide to Understand and Survive Maternal Narcissism is one of the best books I have read on this sensitive topic of maternal narcissism.
--Award Winning Author, Anita Oommen, *Picking up the Shards: Healing the Pain of Mother-Wounds, Discovering the Mother-Heart of God*

A brilliantly written book that addresses a unique trauma. It provided the psychological antidote I have wanted for a long time. Diane Metcalf writes with confidence and clarity and her compassionate voice will be a soothing balm for many broken and hurting hearts.
--Romuald Dzemo, TheBookCommentary.com

Lemon Moms

A Guide to Understand and Survive

Maternal Narcissism

Diane Metcalf

For more information, email Diane@DianeMetcalf.com

Cover design by Diane Metcalf and Christos Angelidakis.

ISBN: 978-1-7352876-7-6

FREE GIFT

To get the best experience possible from this book, I invite you to sign up for the free 8-week e-mail Survival Course.

Register here:

dianemetcalf.com/freerecoverycourse

GET THE FREE APP!

The Toolbox for Healing
Recover from Hurtful People and Relationships!

Information, emotional support, and validation whenever you need it!

Google Play: https://bit.ly/3361PWD
App Store: https://apple.co/3hxrivM

DEDICATION

This book is dedicated to the three most important people in my life:

To my kids, Christin and Matthew, two of the kindest, most accepting, and loving people I know. You bore the brunt of my unresolved codependency, you taught me how to be a mom, and you showed me how to love.

To my adoring husband, and sounding board, Kim, whose unwavering love, support, and encouragement helped to make this book a reality.

Contents

"There are so many kinds of mother. The mothers you cherish and celebrate. The mothers who were never really there. The mothers who broke you. Who built you. The mothers who cheered you on. Who chipped away at you until you were dust. The mothers who reveled in your astonishing intelligence and grace and power. The mothers who died painfully young. The mothers who lived so long you felt yourself disintegrating with them. Petal by wilted petal. The mothers who shined. Who dimmed. Who did their best. Who disappointed. Who redeemed themselves. Who accepted your redemption. Who zigged and zagged. The mothers who were always there. Or never showed up. The mothers who sewed themselves into the quilt you became. The mothers who couldn't bear to say. The mothers who didn't know who they were without you. Who never saw you no matter how wildly you waved. The mothers who grieved you. Who believed in you. The mothers you call. The mothers you eat dinner with. The dead mothers. The mothers you have to search for and carry. The mothers you find in people who are not your mother. The mothers like a limb of yours. The mothers you wish. The mothers you love. The mothers you ache. The mothers you echo. The mothers you became. I am thinking of you. I am loving you all."

—Cheryl Strayed

INTRODUCTION

For as long as I can remember, there was something "different" about my mother. She wasn't like other mothers I knew.

By the time I was middle school-aged, I'd met a lot of moms, and I'd witnessed their interactions with their kids – at parks, the public pool, in stores, at the playground, fast food places, school events, and in their homes. My mom didn't act like them; she didn't relate to me the way they did with their kids. She didn't hug or kiss me. She didn't smile at, spend time with, or play with me. She didn't seem happy to see me. She didn't ask about my school day, and she wasn't interested in knowing my friends. She didn't go to parent-teacher conferences unless I begged. She seemed to have no interest in me or anything that I did.

There were no boundaries in our home. I stayed up as late as I wanted. I wasn't required to do chores, though I was shamed for not doing them. I was expected to care for my younger siblings, and I was blamed and sometimes punished for their misbehavior.

My mom called me hurtful names and obscenities. She struck my face and body with her hands and other objects, and at times she completely ignored me for days, weeks, and even months at a time.

In dysfunctional families, there's an unspoken rule don't talk, don't trust, don't feel. At some point, as an adult, I decided I was done living by those rules, and eventually, I found a path to recovery. I embarked on an ongoing journey of discovery to find healing and peace.

Today my mother is 83 and lives in a memory care facility. She's not the same person I've described in these pages. She's dependent, frail and childlike. She requires a level of care comparable to that of a toddler. Her short-term memory lasts only a matter of seconds. She hallucinates frequently and spends many of her waking hours reliving years gone by.

It's difficult to watch her navigate her world, where she simultaneously lives in the past and present. She has no grasp of time or place. She's no longer the mother I knew. I've discovered a new sense of compassion for her. Sometimes it's hard to believe that this woman, once a force to be reckoned with, can get lost inside of her mind the way that she does. It's a terrible thing to observe.

I know that given her lack of education, unstable support system, abusive upbringing, and limited resources, there wasn't much of an opportunity for her to learn or grow beyond her childhood experiences. I think that she did the best she could with what she had. I think that's all any of us can do.

I hold no ill will, and I wish her the best that life has to offer. I forgave her long ago.

If any part of this sounds like your mother or your relationship with her, you're not alone. If there's a pattern of manipulation, ongoing power struggles, gaslighting, or cruelty in your relationship, this book can help. If you find yourself second-guessing your memory, doubting your judgment, or sanity, or you're continually seeking your mother's withheld affection, attention, or approval, this book can explain why.

Your mother doesn't need a formal "diagnosis" in order for you to determine that your relationship with her is unhealthy. If it is, you can do something about it.

Your mom may not be the mother you want, but she is the mother you have. Until now, you had two choices: live on her terms (focusing on her and chasing after her love and support) or go "no contact." I suggest that you have a third option: allow me to walk with you through the chaos and confusion that is maternal narcissism. I'll show you how to decode the crazy-making behavior, heal the damage, take back your personal power, and move forward to live your best life.

* * *

This book has the potential to be emotionally triggering. If you find that any of the descriptions, memories, thoughts, and experiences shared here cause you to feel anger, sadness, or to recall painful childhood memories, it's a pretty good indication that you've found a resource that can help you.

I hope that you'll begin learning about, understanding, processing, and healing the trauma that you experienced growing up with a toxic parent.

Hang in there.

Diane

PART I
STRONG, DEEP ROOTS

Lemon tree, very pretty, and the lemon flower is sweet
But the fruit of the poor lemon is impossible to eat

— Folk song by Will Holt

THE BEGINNING

"Long-term narcissistic abuse shrinks the hippocampus, which is the part of the brain that is responsible for memory and learning. The amygdalae, areas of the brain responsible for "primitive" emotions like fear, grief, guilt, envy, and shame, become overactive and enlarged from the abuse."

—Katja Wingenfeld and Oliver T. Wolf,
Stress, Memory, and the Hippocampus

It was all about my mother. It was all about how I reflected on her and how I made her look in front of her audience. It was about how she appeared in her role as a mother, and she wanted to be seen as Mother of the Year.

Ugh.

As a child, if we were visiting friends or family and they put out snacks or treats, I knew I was not allowed to help myself or politely ask for any, and I was expected to refuse it if offered. I was not allowed to ask questions, show initiative, or curiosity. Asking questions or taking action meant that I was challenging her or distrusting her. So instead, I was expected to listen, obey, stay quiet, and be the epitome of social decorum, etiquette, and politeness.

These rules were laid down early and enforced aggressively. I was supposed to be the perfect and well-behaved child that would cause other mothers to feel jealous. Mother wanted to be envied.

I was not even in kindergarten yet, and I was terrified of her.

If we went anywhere, she dressed me formally and beautifully—a clean dress, hair combs and barrettes or braids and ponytails; lace anklets and shiny patent leather shoes; and sometimes short, white gloves. I was expected to smile, be soft-spoken, use manners, answer questions but never ask them, and always, ALWAYS make her look *good*. I felt like a toy doll or a puppet rather than a person.

She often stated that children should be seen and not heard.

If I embarrassed her in any way, I knew there would be undesirable consequences. She consistently used threats of physical violence and punishment, such as beating me with "the belt," or breaking my fingers, or killing me. I believed she would do these things, and I lived in fear of doing the "right thing," whatever the right thing was at that particular time. Because "the right thing" could and would change haphazardly, depending, it seemed, on a whim, or perhaps nothing at all. All I knew was that I needed to be alert. Vigilant. All the time.

When she was cross with anyone, she angrily took it out on me and called me names that belittled and humiliated. The name-calling hurt me intensely and made me feel like there was something fundamentally unacceptable about me. I felt like I was less of a person. She attacked me with words such as lazy, selfish, pig, liar, glutton, and the biggest insult of all, in her opinion: "You're just like your father." Later, when I was a young teen, she would add "whore" (even though I was a virgin) to her repertoire.

Her manipulation and iron-fisted control started early in my life, but the verbal and physical mistreatment didn't begin until I was eight years old.

My father left when I was eight, and it began shortly after that.

After he left, my mother used my fear of abandonment to manipulate me. She threatened to give my siblings and me away, put us in an orphanage, or send us to live with our father, whom she repeatedly told us had left us for another woman, and who "didn't love us or want anything to do with us."

Angry, red-faced, eyes bulging, and teeth bared, she shouted, "Why did I have you? I can't wait 'til you grow up and get the hell out!"

Without my father's presence, I felt lost and alone. Nobody was there to look out for me. I needed this strange new way of existing without him to make sense. I determined that my mother's new nastiness was the result of her anger toward my dad, or because he was in love with another woman; or because my mother was afraid, alone, lonely, feeling unloved, unwanted, abandoned, angry, rejected, and most of all because she wanted him back. I made countless explanations and excuses for her behavior, all along, hoping he would come back.

But he didn't.

With him gone, it was like she had been given a free pass to express herself in any hurtful way she wanted.

Throughout my childhood, I never heard anything resembling, "I see you." "I hear you." "How are you?" "How was your day?" "What did you learn in school today?" "What's new?" "Have fun!" She wasn't emotionally present in my life. It felt like she didn't care, and I felt alone in the world.

I was empathetic and understood that she was hurting. I somehow believed I was emotionally stronger than she was, even at this very young age. I was convinced I could take whatever brutality she dispensed. I thought it was temporary. Besides, what choice did I have? And so, the trauma bonding and codependency began.

Trauma bonds are powerful emotional bonds between two individuals who undergo cycles of abuse together. Over time, trauma bonds become very resistant to change, and a codependent relationship forms.

Codependency develops when someone takes responsibility, blame, or makes excuses for another person's harmful or hurtful behavior.

Throughout my childhood and young adult life at home, I witnessed ongoing narcissistic rages and rantings. (Narcissistic rage is defined as intense anger, aggression, or even passive aggression that narcissists exhibit when they experience anything that triggers feelings of incompetence, vulnerability, or shame. When their fantasies of superiority are challenged, rage results. I'll talk about rages in depth later on.)

Over the ensuing years after my dad's departure, I got to hear the latest and greatest versions of her story, entitled "Poor Me." The story was always about her victimhood, her innocence, and her betrayal by my father. I heard various descriptions of what an awful man my father was, about his inability to love anyone but himself, and about his selfishness, lies, deceit, and adultery and how he never wanted us. But the father I knew was loving, kind, and caring and obviously loved me very much. All that while, I created stories for myself, so that the discrepancies made sense. I wanted to believe we were just like any other family.

During these elementary school years, my mom parented by blaming, shaming, intimidating, threatening, and physically punishing. There were frequent struggles for control over what I ate. I had a glass of milk dumped over my head because I said I didn't want it after it had been poured. Another time, I was forced to take my dinner into the cold, dark attic when I was no longer hungry and couldn't finish. I was terrified of the attic, and she knew it. She knew of my intense dislike for beets and yet forced me to eat them under threat of violence, such that I vomited them immediately onto my dinner plate. Then I was punished for that by being sent to my room. I was reminded daily that children were starving in other parts of the world and that I should eat "what was in front of me" whether I liked it or not. I failed to see the relationship between these statements. She seemed to be saying that by eating, I could somehow alleviate the suffering of starving children. This didn't make sense to me. Maybe she should just send them my food? I didn't understand until I was much older that she wanted and expected me to express gratitude for the food she provided, and that she was insulted when I wasn't hungry, didn't like the food, or the way it was prepared.

As her angry outbursts and bizarre punishments continued, I learned throughout these early years that I was always somehow to blame. I was challenging her rules, not meeting her uncommunicated expectations, or blatantly ungrateful. So you see, I was directly responsible for her anger and deserved the punishment! At the same time, there seemed to be no sense or logic to what might set her off. It was like living with an unpredictable animal that could hurt me any time it chose, for any reason or no reason. I could never predict the amount of rage she'd release on me or the degree of punishment. It felt like no matter what I did, it was always the wrong choice. I was left feeling unsafe, distrustful, and wary. I felt like I couldn't do anything right, and second-guessing and doubting myself became the norm. If I cried because of the overwhelming confusion or sense of defeat, she'd mock me or tell me that I had no reason to feel or act that way.

Feeling guilty for doing anything that could upset my mother or cause her to focus on me, I continually made myself unnoticeable by staying out of her way as much as possible. I felt like a burden, making her life harder simply because I existed. The seeds of unworthiness had been sown.

I started feeling liable for her emotional and sometimes physical well-being, and I took responsibility for them. Over time, she came to expect it. She shared her thoughts and feelings with me in frightening, highly emotionally charged, biased, and inappropriate ways. So, at the age of twelve, gaslighting, and cognitive dissonance had already become a way of life. My training for becoming an "Enabler-Extraordinaire" had begun.

"Gaslighting" is a term from the 1938 stage play *Gaslight*. In the story, a husband attempts to drive his wife insane by dimming their home's gas-powered lights and denying it when his wife notices. This causes her to doubt her perception, judgment, memory, and reality. She begins to believe she's losing her mind.

When you're gaslighted, especially if you're a child, you don't know what's happening. You're primarily confused, stressed, and frustrated, and you can't figure out the reason. Gaslighting gives a narcissist mother a *tremendous* amount of power and control over her child.

Cognitive dissonance is the confusion and mental discomfort you experience when living with contradictory beliefs, ideas, or values.

Throughout this book, I talk about very personal, highly emotionally charged topics, some of which may cause you to feel uncomfortable. You might also begin to remember events you assumed you'd forgotten.

This book prepares you for healing. You see, to heal entirely and for good, you have to remember and, to some degree, re-experience the childhood trauma, but as an adult this time so you understand it on an adult level. To heal, you must take this understanding, validate how someone else's narcissism affected you, reframe those experiences now as an adult, and move forward.

I recommend getting yourself a journal or notebook. Be selective about it. Invest in it. Your journal should be something that calls to you and speaks to your heart. Personalize it and make it a beautiful place to write your thoughts and feelings as you work through this book.

The journal is a private and personal space only for you; it's for your eyes only. It's your safe place to reflect upon your reading, learning, thinking, and feeling. No one is going to read, judge, or grade your journal. Use it to write what's in your heart. Its purpose is to help you work through the more challenging aspects of creating awareness, in a safe emotional space, where healing can truly begin. You could use the *Lemon Moms: Companion Workbook* in place of a journal. The workbook has "Takeaway's," additional "Action for Healing" questions, and spaces for you to write and reflect. It's available for purchase on Amazon.com.

Chapter One
WHAT IS NARCISSISM?

"Narcissism falls along the axis of what psychologists called personality disorders, one of a group that includes antisocial, dependent, histrionic, avoidant, and borderline personalities. But by most measures, narcissism is one of the worst, if only because the narcissist themselves are so clueless."

—Jeffrey Kluger

If you're "Googling," reading, and researching, trying to find information or reasons for your mother's hurtful behavior and what to do about it, it could be that she's on the narcissism spectrum. But what exactly is narcissism?

At an American Psychoanalytic Association meeting held in February 2018, the topic of narcissism generated presentations, a large number of papers, and much discussion. Zlatan Krizan and Anne Herlache of Iowa State University pointed out that researchers commonly disagree about narcissism's key features and how they're structured. They observed that the definition of narcissism focuses on qualities like grandiosity and self-glorification, but that it also includes a level of vulnerability and insecurity. These contradictory features "have awkwardly co-existed throughout the history of the construct." As a result, Krizan and Herlache define narcissism basically as "entitled self-importance" (2018).

In this chapter, we'll learn about some specific personality traits and the associated behaviors that define narcissistic personality disorder (NPD).

The characteristics of narcissistic personality disorder were first described in 1925 by an Austrian psychoanalyst named Robert Waelder. But the clinical term "narcissistic personality disorder" was actually coined more recently in the 1970s by an Austrian-American psychoanalyst, Heinz Kohut. Kohut is known for his theories on developing a healthy sense of self (O'Donohue and William 2007; Kohut and Heinz 1968).

NPD is recognized by a publication of the American Psychiatric Association known as the "Diagnostic and Statistical Manual of Mental Disorders" (DSM). The DSM is the authority and official source for the definitions of mental illnesses and their diagnoses as well as possible treatments. It is used by clinicians to diagnose mental disorders in children and adults.

"NPD is one of the least studied personality disorders. It appears to be prevalent, highly comorbid with other psychiatric disorders and associated with significant psychosocial disability. NPD is challenging to treat and can complicate the treatment of co-occurring disorders."

—Caligor and Petrini 2018

NPD often exists with other mental disorders (Paris 2014). It's also associated with comorbidly (simultaneously) occurring with bipolar, anorexia, and substance use disorders. In the United States, about 0.5 percent (or 1 in 200 people) have this disorder. There is a difference according to gender: about 75 percent of those with NPD are men (Weinheimer, J., Russo, J., Giblock, D., & Kuber, J. 2020).

NPD is considered one of the four cluster B personality disorders, according to the DSM-5. In addition to NPD, cluster B includes antisocial personality disorder (ASPD), borderline personality disorder (BPD), and histrionic personality disorder (HPD). NPD has similarities with the other cluster B disorders, which are characterized by drama and/or unreliable, very emotional behavior, impulse control, and lack of emotional regulation (Hoermann, Zupanick, and Dombeck 2019).

People with NPD can:

- become impatient and angry when they don't receive the treatment they expect;

- have difficulty relating to others;

- feel slighted or insulted very easily;

- react with anger, contempt, and belittling to make themselves look superior;

- have trouble controlling their emotions and behavior;

- find it challenging to deal with stress or adapt to changes;

- feel secretly depressed because they're not perfect; and

- feel insecure, ashamed, and vulnerable.

People who have narcissistic personality disorder (narcissists) have a distorted self-image.

Narcissists are often described as "challenging" to interact with. They can be defensive and condescending and believe they "know everything." The appearance of having prestige, power, and superiority is vital to them, and they're susceptible to criticism and feelings of shame. As a result, they'll protect their sense of self at any cost, and that can include being aggressive and physically abusive. Narcissists' emotions are often unstable and intense and out of proportion to the situation at hand. Additionally, narcissists can be envious and manipulative and exhibit a noticeable lack of empathy or caring about the well-being of others.

Narcissism has no known cure, but narcissists don't usually seek any help or therapy anyway because they don't think they need it. If they seek treatment, it's generally because it's been requested (or mandated) by a third party or is personally sought because of interpersonal or professional difficulty or conflict.

NPD Personality Traits

- Concerned with image and status

- Don't like accountability or taking responsibility

- Prone to rages when they feel threatened

- Comfortable using violence to achieve goals

- Manipulative

- Test boundaries to see how far they can go

- Impatient

- Easily frustrated

- Irritable

- Can't communicate honestly because "winning" is the goal

- Invalidate others' feelings

- Indifferent

- Unapologetic

- Place blame on others

- Shirk personal responsibility

- Use name-calling and public humiliation to control others

- Hostile

- Aggressive

- Selfish, self-centered

- Unable to identify with other people's feelings

- Lack of compassion and remorse

- Words don't match their actions. In my experience: her words didn't match her intonation or facial expressions. Example: she gives a compliment in a sarcastic tone or while eye-rolling. This is called a "mixed message" (Stines 2019)

- Use cognitive empathy rather than emotional empathy

NPD Behaviors

- "Rewrite history" to protect their image. This is also an aspect of "gaslighting." In their version of the story, they're either the hero or the victim.

- Staring at you, to make you uncomfortable

- Baiting you/picking fights

- Emotional dumping (expecting you to listen to their problems, criticisms of you, how you disappoint them, and what or how you should change to please them.) Dumping is done without empathy. They have no regard for how this will affect you, and they won't allow you to share your feelings; it is a single-sided interaction. They're not interested in how you feel.

- Intentionally misunderstanding, or "twisting" words to give them a different meaning

- Projecting thoughts or feelings onto you and saying it's how *you* think or feel

- Threatening to publicly shame or "ruin" you by publishing something embarrassing such as a picture or letter

- Expecting behavior or a level of understanding from children that isn't age-appropriate

- Expecting emotional caretaking

- View life as a game of power and control; they play to win at any cost

- Use other people's empathy and vulnerability against them

- Experience narcissistic rages: showing intense anger, aggression, or passive aggression when experiencing anything that shatters their illusion of grandiosity, entitlement, or superiority, or triggers feelings of inadequacy, shame, or vulnerability

- Coercion: Getting you to give up something you want, or to do something you don't want to do

Narcissists are a type of "high-conflict personality." They exhibit behaviors that most of us would never do, such as thoughtlessly spending other people's money, humiliating a child in public, sabotaging a coworker, or verbally attacking a waitress (Eddy 2018).

They consider themselves superior and are comfortable with "putting down," insulting, and demeaning others in order to feel powerful or boost their self-image. They tend to be selfish and do not reciprocate kind gestures or invitations. They're demanding, needing almost constant admiration and attention from anyone in their vicinity.

Additionally, they waste time trying to impress anyone who will listen to them; they break promises, make excuses, take credit for others' ideas or work. They enjoy bullying and are willing to speak disapprovingly of someone behind their back but have only positive things to say in their presence. All of these traits can make narcissists exhausting for those of us who live and work with them.

WHY IS EMPATHY IMPORTANT?

Empathy, or specifically, the lack thereof, is a narcissism trait. When talking about narcissism, it's crucial to understand what is meant by the term "empathy" and the role it plays in the relationship dynamics of a narcissist. A person's lack of empathy is a big red flag.

The "empathy gene" was first referenced in research published in the journal *Translational Psychiatry* on March 12, 2018. To date, this was the most extensive genetic study done on empathy. It found that the degree of empathy any of us have is at least partly due to genetics.

There's still a lot of discussion and debate regarding whether narcissists have any empathy and whether they can feel emotions like guilt or remorse.

It's commonly understood in the field of social psychology that there are two kinds of empathy: *cognitive* and *emotional*. When we feel an emotion that someone else is feeling, it's known as emotional empathy, the ability to put ourselves in another person's place and feel what they're feeling. If you see someone crying, and it makes you feel sad, you're experiencing emotional empathy.

Emotional empathy requires:

- Feeling the same emotion as another person (For example, seeing someone embarrass themselves and then feeling embarrassed for them.)

- Feeling distressed in response to another person's feelings

- Feeling compassion for another person

Having *emotional empathy* can be extremely distressing for us. When we feel pain resulting from somebody else's emotions, that experience can immobilize us. There's a balance to be sought and maintained when it comes to feeling for others and not letting our empathy negatively affect our own lives.

Cognitive empathy is the ability to have an intellectual understanding that someone may be feeling a particular emotion and not feeling anything in response to this knowledge. Narcissists can see another's perspective and then respond in the manner that best benefits them. Doing this requires a rudimentary understanding and some basic knowledge about emotions (Hodges and Myers, 2007).

Narcissists are more likely to use cognitive empathy rather than emotional empathy, and it's essential to understand this dynamic (Baskin-Sommers, Krusemark, and Ronningstam 2014).

When a narcissist uses a simple visual perspective to guess what someone's feeling, they're using cognitive empathy. In other words, if they can look at a person and notice that their eyes are swollen and red, possibly from crying, they may correctly guess that the person is feeling sad. This type of empathy has nothing to do with actually feeling anything themselves. So, if a narcissist knows someone well enough, they can guess how that person feels, and they'll also have a pretty good idea of how to use that information to hurt that individual too.

Daniel Goleman (author of the book "Emotional Intelligence"), writes in his blog that torturers need to have a good sense of "cognitive empathy" to figure out how to hurt a person best.

Similarly, if a narcissist acts kindly, what they may actually be doing is feeling around for hopes, wishes, and dreams to use later to inflict pain intentionally.

THE EGO, SELF, AND FALSE SELF

The word "ego" is Latin, meaning "I." It is the conscious part of us that makes decisions. It mediates between our own desires and those of society, hopefully keeping them in a healthy balance (Leary 2019). "Ego" became a household word after 1894 with the popularity of the Austrian neurologist and psychologist Sigmund Freud (1856–1939). Freud is considered to be one of the most influential thinkers of the twentieth century and is recognized as the father of modern psychoanalysis

The "ego" is the part of the mind that organizes our thoughts so we can understand and remember them, and it makes sense of our environment, expressing our mental capacity, memory, understanding of reality, and other mental functions. The ego decides what's real and what isn't; it's the referee between the conscious and the unconscious minds. Our ego is responsible for our sense of self, our personal identity, and is also the filter through which we see ourselves. We tell our egos "stories" that help justify our thoughts and beliefs about who we are (Snowden and Ruth 2006). The ego is frequently thought of as the "self."

Carl Jung (1875–1961), the Swiss psychiatrist, psychoanalyst, and founder of analytical psychology, says that the ego is not the self. Instead, the self includes the ego, as well as the conscious and unconscious minds. To him, the self is the total personality, and the ego is only a small part of the self.

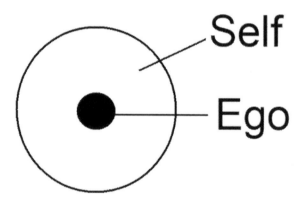

Using a "circle within a circle" to represent this idea, the self is the bigger circle, and the ego is a smaller circle in the center. (Lawson 2008; Zweig 1991).

Using Jung's premise, the (true) self is the part of us that recognizes and experiences our feelings and desires. In this book, the terms "ego" and "self" are distinct, well-defined, and not intended to be used interchangeably. This book is written from Jung's perspective that the self is not the ego, but that it includes the ego, as shown in the diagram above.

The idea that narcissists have true and false selves was first proposed by the American physician and psychotherapist Alexander Lowen (1910–2008).

The "false self" (also known as "false face") is an image that narcissists develop during early life. It changes and adapts over time, acting as a shield against pain and *narcissistic injury*, which is anything the narcissist perceives as a threat to their false self, or to their sense of importance and dominance. Narcissists repeatedly revise their false face in terms of their basic needs, relationships, and conduct to continue protecting and hiding the true self. In doing this, the false self becomes the familiar and public face that others believe to be the narcissists' true self.

When a person functions from within their false self, they experience a feeling of disconnectedness from their genuine emotions and how they would typically relate to others. When using this false face, narcissists respond the way *they think they should* feel or are *supposed to feel* or *want to feel,* instead of how they actually do. Subsequently, only those closest to the narcissist are aware of this discrepancy. All others are only allowed to see the public image or false face. Still, those closest to the narcissist witness and experience the narcissist's true self, and they regularly observe and interact with both faces firsthand. This is what makes talking about the narcissist with others who only know the false face so frustrating.

The false face can imitate emotions and empathy, and this is great for the narcissist because it allows them to appear as kind, caring, and compassionate individuals. Secretly, the false face is threatened by anything perceived as criticism, and narcissists are terribly concerned with how other people think about and understand them. This false self is typically anxious, judgmental, and insecure overall. At the same time, it believes it's more acceptable and lovable than the real self could ever be. Narcissists don't like themselves and can't accept their true selves. That's why their false face must be kept intact, and the way they do this is called "obtaining narcissistic supply." We'll get into that topic later on.

"Narcissists lack the ability to emotionally tune in to other people. They cannot feel and show empathy or unconditional love. They are typically critical and judgmental."

—Karyl McBride

Most narcissists will never know whether they're on the NPD spectrum or have full-blown NPD. Most don't seek treatment and will never have the benefit of a professional diagnosis because they don't think they have a problem. They believe their problems are all caused by others, and they don't accept personal responsibility. They are blamers. So, most narcissists will never see their own role in any of their interpersonal problems.

Takeaways

- A "false face" is a coping mechanism formed during childhood. It changes and adapts over time, acting as a shield against pain and narcissistic injury.

- Narcissists display personality traits, such as selfishness, vanity, manipulation, and self-importance. They're often defensive, condescending, and "know everything." They can be aggressive and even physically abusive and are challenging when interacting with them.

- Most narcissists will never know whether they're on the NPD spectrum or have full-blown NPD because they don't seek treatment.

Action for Healing

The first step in healing is acknowledging that you grew up in a dysfunctional family. You may be reluctant to do this because it's painful, and it stirs up memories that you'd rather keep buried. If these statements are true for you, I encourage you to go at your own pace, making notes in your journal and giving yourself time and space for self-reflection and beginning the healing process.

1. Do any of the NPD behaviors and personality traits feel familiar to you? Write about this in your journal: How are they familiar? As you write, stay aware of your emotions and how you're feeling. Make a note of your feelings as they come: Are you feeling surprised? Shocked? Unsure? Defensive? Sad? Angry? In

denial? Write about *each* emotion you feel. Write about your memories as you remember them—not as you may have been told that they happened.

2. Using what you just wrote, focus *less* on what your mother said or did, and *more* on how you felt. If you can remember them, make a list of the feelings you were experiencing at the time when this or that thing happened. For example, I wrote, "I felt scared out of my mind when you screamed and yelled at me because your face turned purple, and your eyes bulged out, making you look insane. Your voice was so loud it hurt my ears and vibrated in my chest. You looked and sounded like a monster to me, and I thought you might physically hurt or kill me."

3. Look over everything you just wrote. Acknowledge that you felt those emotions and that you *had the right to feel them*. Say it aloud: "I felt ____ and ____, and ____ and I had reason to feel those emotions. I lived with this. I witnessed this. It was real."

You are validating *yourself* when you acknowledge your feelings. You are *acknowledging* the fact that you were x years old with big, scary feelings that you may not have known the words for. You were probably confused. If you couldn't tell anyone about these feelings or what was causing them, you probably felt like you had no choice but to keep them bottled up inside. You may have re-experienced these same feelings at other times in your life when you found yourself in similar situations. Let yourself cry if you feel like it. It's OK to feel your feelings. You're in a safe space.

Chapter Two
CREATING A NARCISSIST

"The greater a child's terror, and the earlier it is experienced, the harder it becomes to develop a strong and healthy sense of self."

—Nathaniel Branden, Six Pillars of Self-Esteem

How Does Narcissism Start?

Psychologists say that narcissism often begins with early childhood trauma via a narcissistic parent or caregiver. So it's entirely possible that as children, our mothers were targets of narcissists.

As children, we cope the best that we know how, with the skills we have at the time, healthy or not. Some kids learn to deal with the trauma of living with a narcissist by imitating that narcissist and eventually becoming one themselves. They may take a different approach to deal with narcissistic wounding, and learn to please and placate the narcissist, developing codependent coping skills in the process. Codependent children take these maladaptive skills with them into adulthood, as "codependents."

Codependency is an emotional and behavioral coping style. It affects one's ability to have healthy, satisfying relationships. It's a set of learned behaviors that can be passed down through generations through modeling. Codependent individuals rely on other people for their sense of identity, approval, and affirmation because they haven't learned how to do this for themselves. They are "people pleasers" who are willing to play by the "rules" of others, losing their own identity in the process. Codependency is often a result of some type of ongoing mistreatment or abuse. This kind of self-abandonment can cause codependent individuals to suppress anger and become depressed, anxious, or experience panic disorders. It can lead to self-doubt, low self-esteem, lack of energy, or feelings of helplessness, hopelessness, powerlessness, and defeat. We'll talk at length about codependency in later chapters.

THE IMPORTANCE OF CAREGIVERS

When a primary caregiver is a narcissist, kids are vulnerable to becoming targets of narcissistic maltreatment and abuse. Children don't have the mental capacity to understand that their parent is mentally ill. They completely trust and depend upon their parents, and the result is that they don't question what they're told. Because of this, children can be easily manipulated and emotionally controlled.

All children need their parents' approval and affirmation. If they grow up in a home environment that's highly competitive or where love is conditional, they begin to realize that they have to be "the best" to be loved and appreciated. They understand that they need to earn their parents' love and support by "achieving." The feelings of inadequacy the child feels from not being "good enough" may be the catalyst that starts the development of a false self.

If a home environment is such that one parent is emotionally unstable, it can cause the children to experience a sense of almost daily drama, with resulting feelings of insecurity, instability, and fear. If one parent is threatening, angry, or verbally abusive, the children's roles in the family will change according to that parent's emotional state. The children will take turns being devalued and idealized by that parent, according to the children's achievements or lack thereof. These family dynamics are such that everyone revolves around the explosive or unstable parent, trying to please or placate them and to remain in good standing as long as possible. The children respond in their own individual and unique ways, developing feelings of anger and becoming rebellious or developing a deep sense of shame or of not being "good enough," suffering from low self-esteem. Yet, other children may feel defeated and just give up, becoming withdrawn or depressed, or self-isolating. Still, others learn to hide their imperfections by developing a false self and adopting the values and characteristics of the narcissistic parent (Greenberg 2016).

If your mother has been diagnosed with NPD or has NPD characteristics, she may have created a false self during childhood. She protects that false image fiercely because it's everything that her true self is not. From her perspective, the false self is preferable to the real self. The true self is "lacking;" the false self is not. To survive emotionally, she would use the false self to hide and protect her true self.

As we've seen, narcissists enjoy believing they're superior, smarter, and better at everything than everybody else. This is one of the reasons they're often defensive and anger so easily and quickly. If you challenge a narcissist, there will usually be crazy-making repercussions, and as children of narcissists, we understand that very well.

Narcissistic parents are not healthy role models for their children. They find no issue with using foul language in front of or even directed at their children. They may make age-inappropriate adult/sexual statements, inferences, or jokes in front of or to their children. They generally behave immaturely, impulsively, and may openly express their addictions. They may violate the law to get what they want. This kind of behavior was a regular occurrence in our house—my mother making embarrassing and inappropriate sexual jokes and innuendos in front of my friends and me when I was a pre-teen. During my teen years, she flirted with my male friends or boyfriends, and openly expressed her belief that they were sexually attracted to her. When I was sixteen, she and my maternal aunt asked me to accompany them to a pornographic movie at a remote theater late at night. At the time, I thought this was a completely normal mother's request for her teenage daughter.

Narcissist parents are oblivious to the damage they inflict on their children when they expose them to inappropriate situations and behaviors. They're not self-aware enough to see how their actions affect others.

Takeaways

- Narcissism often begins in early childhood as a result of trauma caused by a narcissistic parent or caregiver. The "false face" is a coping mechanism that was formed during that time.

- Some kids deal with the trauma by imitating their narcissist caretaker and becoming a narcissist as a result or by pleasing and placating and becoming codependent.

- Kids are vulnerable to becoming targets of narcissistic abuse.

- Narcissistic parents are oblivious to the damage they inflict on their children.

Action for Healing

1. How do you feel when you realize your mother might have been a narcissist's target when she was a child? Are you surprised? Do you feel sad? Angry? Explore and journal your feelings about this possibility.

2. If she was a narcissist's target, could that explain her current way of behaving and relating to you now? Why or why not? What do you know about her childhood? Write about it.

Chapter Three
DIAGNOSTIC CRITERIA

"Trauma is personal. It does not disappear if it is not validated. When it is ignored or invalidated, the silent screams continue internally heard only by the one held captive. When someone enters the pain and hears the screams, healing can begin."

—Danielle Bernock, *Emerging With Wings:*
A True Story of Lies, Pain, and the Love that Heals

In these first chapters, we've taken a look at what narcissism is. In this chapter, we'll learn how it's diagnosed.

The "Diagnostic and Statistical Manual of Mental Disorders" (DSM) is a publication by the American Psychiatric Association. This important book is the authority and official source of definitions for mental illnesses, their diagnoses, and possible treatments. It's used by clinicians to diagnose mental disorders in children and adults.

Personality disorders consist of long-term patterns of behavior, making them more commonly diagnosed during adulthood. When someone has NPD, they display a limited yet persistent behavior pattern that repeats itself.

Personality disorders like narcissistic personality disorder are usually diagnosed by a mental health professional, often a psychologist or psychiatrist. Other doctors, such as general practitioners or family doctors, are not sufficiently trained to make a psychological diagnosis. These doctors make referrals to mental health professionals for diagnosis and treatment.

Diagnosing NPD

To make a diagnosis, the mental health professional takes the person's life history, the current state of being (relationship issues, conflicts, etc.), and emotional/behavioral symptoms into account. They look at the big picture to determine whether these symptoms meet five of the nine criteria as determined by the DSM.

Individuals who have NPD may present it in many ways, some of which appear to conflict. For example, a narcissist may be grandiose or insecure, may have high levels of self-confidence or have low self-esteem, or be loud and obnoxious or quiet and manipulative. It's been a long-standing topic of discussion among mental health professionals as to how individuals presenting with such widely differing traits could all have the same diagnosis.

The most recent iteration of the DSM, known as the fifth edition, *DSM-5*, or *DSM-V*, was written in 2013, and diagnostic confusion still abounds about NPD's variable presentations and wide range of severity. The proposed new criteria and empirically-based thresholds in the *DSM-5* were supposed to take care of these issues (Skodol, Bender, and Morey 2014; Krizan and Herlache 2018).

Although the *DSM-5* was proposed to be a "new model" for diagnosing personality disorders that would use a hybrid approach (based on personality-functioning *and* pathological personality traits), the criteria haven't changed from those in *DSM-4*. While a "new model" for diagnosis is included in the *DSM-5*, it's relegated to a separate section.

It's called "the alternative model," and is considered an "alternative for further study."

According to the *DSM-5,* the definition of NPD (301.81) is "a pervasive pattern of grandiosity (in fantasy or behavior,) need for admiration, beginning by early adulthood and present in a variety of contexts, as indicated by five or more of nine criteria" (669).

NINE CRITERIA

The nine criteria for diagnosing narcissistic personality disorder all emphasize feelings of superiority, displays of arrogance, and beliefs of being unique. To be diagnosed with NPD, at least five of the following nine traits need to be present:

1. A grandiose sense of self-importance (For example, "exaggerates achievements and talents, expects to be recognized as superior without commensurate achievements").

2. Fantasies of unlimited success, power, brilliance, beauty, or ideal love.

3. A belief that he or she is special and unique and "can only be understood by, or should associate with, other special or high-status people (or institutions)."

4. A need for "excessive admiration."

5. A sense of entitlement (For example, "unreasonable expectations of especially favorable treatment or automatic compliance with his or her expectations").

6. Interpersonally exploitive behavior (For example, "takes advantage of others to achieve his or her own ends").

7. A lack of empathy and, as such, is "unwilling to recognize or identify with the feelings and needs of others."

8. Envy of others or a belief that others are envious of him or her.

9. A demonstration of arrogant and haughty behaviors or attitudes (301.81).

For those of you who are interested, here's a bit of detail regarding possible changes to the diagnostic criteria for NPD in upcoming editions of the DSM.

A NEW MODEL

When they were writing the DSM-5, "the DSM-5 Personality and Personality Disorder Work Group" proposed a new model of personality-related impairment and pathological personality traits. It wasn't accepted, and the DSM-4 model was retained as the official diagnostic system. The proposed new approach was included in the DSM-5, in a section for "emerging measures and models," encouraging "further study." The decision to leave out the proposed new model was based on the limited support that individual components received and the strong disagreement with aspects of the new approach (Few et al. 2013).

The DSM-5 alternative model places great importance on having personal difficulties with self-definition, self-esteem, and emotional regulation. "NPD is characterized by the presence of both grandiosity and attention-seeking" (768).

The alternative model provides a "level of functioning" scale to obtain this data.

The DSM alternative model defines Narcissistic Personality Disorder as characterized by moderate (or more significant) impairment in "personality functioning." Personality functioning is defined as the degree to which the sense of self and interpersonal functioning are intact.

The Alternative Model: Diagnostic Criteria

The criteria to define Narcissistic Personality Disorder using the alternative model are:

A. "Moderate or greater" impairment in personality functioning demonstrated by difficulties in two (or more) of these four areas (bolded):

Self-functioning:

- **Identity** (i.e., Rely on others for self-definition and self-esteem regulation)

- **Self-direction** (i.e., Obtaining other's approval, their own personal standards are unreasonably high or low)

Interpersonal functioning:

- **Empathy** (i.e., Impaired recognition or identification with other's feelings or needs; extremely reaction-seeking if the feelings or needs are perceived as relevant to the self)

- **Intimacy** (i.e., Superficial relationships, exist to serve self-esteem; little genuine interest in others)

B. THE PRESENCE OF *BOTH* OF THE GRANDIOSITY AND ATTENTION-SEEKING PATHOLOGICAL PERSONALITY TRAITS (SKODOL, BENDER, AND MOREY 2014).

The pathological "personality traits" are organized into these five domains:

1. Negative affectivity

2. Detachment

3. Antagonism

    a. **Grandiosity**: Feelings of entitlement, either overt or covert; self-centeredness; firmly holding to the belief that one is better than others; condescending toward others.

    b. **Attention-seeking**: Excessive attempts to attract and be the focus of the attention of others; admiration seeking.

4. Disinhibition

5. Psychoticism (Oldham, 2015).

So, individuals affected by NPD must have difficulty in at least two of the four bulleted areas listed above in bold, AND they must have a sense of grandiosity *and* display attention-seeking behaviors ("a" and "b" in the "Antagonism" domain above.)

The complete section III diagnostic criteria for NPD include C through G of the general criteria for personality disorders and have not been included in an effort to conserve space.

Additionally, the twenty-five specific trait features within the five domains are not listed here. The traits were developed from the reviews of existing trait models as well as new research (Krueger et al. 2012).

As you can see, diagnosing NPD would be a much more difficult and complicated process when using the DSM-5 alternative model. Personally, I hope it's included in the next iteration. It seems it would provide a more thorough diagnosis.

WHAT'S NEXT?

There are currently no blood, laboratory, or genetic tests available to diagnose personality disorders.

"Having a personality disorder or being on the narcissism spectrum doesn't mean a narcissist is a "bad" person, but it does significantly decrease their ability to have mutually satisfying relationships."

Although there is no "cure," long-term outpatient psychoanalytic psychotherapy and medication management is the treatment choice for narcissistic personality disorder. Other forms of treatment include group, family, and couples therapy; cognitive-behavioral therapy (CBT); and short-term objective-focused psychotherapy (Ronningstam and Maltsberger 2007).

It's interesting to note that as a person with NPD ages, their symptoms often decrease in intensity. Many people experience a small number of the most extreme symptoms by the time they reach age fifty. This is true of all personality disorders, and I have seen this with my own mother, as well (Bressert 2019).

TAKEAWAYS

- In the DSM-5, there are nine criteria for diagnosing narcissistic personality disorder. All emphasize feeling superior, having arrogant behavior, and beliefs of being entitled or special.

- To be diagnosed with narcissistic personality disorder (using the current model,) at least five of these traits need to be expressed.

- Narcissists demand attention and admiration, lack empathy, take advantage, and hold a high amount of contempt for others.

- When someone has NPD, they display a limited behavior pattern that repeats itself, regardless of your reaction or response.

ACTION FOR HEALING

1. In your journal, list the things that you learned about narcissism that you didn't know before.

    How has what you've learned impacted your thoughts or feelings about your childhood? This is a tough question. You may feel anger, confusion, guilt, frustration, even hatred. Let yourself feel what you feel without judgment. Validate and accept your feelings.

2. Look over what you just wrote. Acknowledge what you feel. Say aloud, "I feel ___, and ___, and ___."

You are validating *yourself* when you do this. You are *acknowledging* the fact that you feel these feelings and that it's OK to explore them. Feelings come and go. They intensify, and then they wane. Although it's hard, sit with these feelings and remind yourself that you are a human being who is supposed to feel and experience emotions. Acknowledge that "feeling" is a way that we experience life.

3. You might be feeling unforgiving, or like wanting to talk with a counselor or support group. You may desire to rediscover yourself or begin taking better care of yourself.

    Hold yourself. Cry if you want to. Envision the little child that you were back then and talk to them. Tell them that you're here for them now. Let them know that you've learned some things you didn't know before and that they were never to blame for what happened. Tell them that they were always worthy and always good enough. Promise them you'll continue learning and growing and changing and that they'll never have to endure that kind of treatment again. Sooth them and love them the way they should have been loved. This is called "inner child work." If this kind of healing work speaks to you, I think you should pursue it. There are many free resources online that can help with inner-child healing work.

Chapter Four
TYPES OF NARCISSISM

"If you are being mistreated, exploited, or abused by anyone, however, it doesn't matter what type of narcissist they are or even if they're a narcissist at all. Run!"

—Kristen Milstead

So far, we've seen that narcissism is a personality disorder that's diagnosed by qualified mental health practitioners. We've found that narcissism often begins in childhood, and we've looked at the common traits and characteristics of narcissistic behavior.

In this chapter, we'll learn to recognize two types and two subtypes of narcissism as they're defined in the DSM-5.

Narcissism occurs along a spectrum, meaning that for each individual, there are more and less severe forms of the disorder.

A study was done in 2015, *Narcissistic Personality Disorder: Diagnostic and Clinical Challenges*, which indicated *grandiose* and *vulnerable* narcissism as the two main types (Caligor, Levy, and Yeomans 2015). Each of these two types of narcissism has its own set of traits and characteristics, and each has its own way of protecting its sense of self.

There are two subcategories of these types which distinguish *how* grandiose and vulnerable narcissists get their emotional and egotistical needs met. These are the *overt* and *covert* subtypes of NPD (Milstead 2018).

Let's take a look at each of these types and subtypes.

GRANDIOSE NARCISSISM

"Grandiose" narcissism is the textbook type of narcissism that comes to mind when most people hear the term "narcissism." It's also known as high-functioning, exhibitionist, or classic narcissism. These narcissists are extroverted, dominant, and always seem to be pursuing power and prestige. They believe that they're a step above everyone else, that they're smarter, better-looking, and more powerful. Grandiose narcissists brag about themselves and will put down others as a way to raise their feelings of self-importance. They're often rude, insensitive, and even cruel. They ignore, are unaware of, or don't care about how their behavior affects others.

In the case of narcissistic mothers, they view their children as extensions of themselves rather than as people in their own right with thoughts, feelings, perceptions, goals, ideas, dreams, and desires of their own. For narcissistic moms, children are a means for obtaining admiration and validation. As we've seen, the false face behaves socially acceptably and imitates empathy. This makes narcissistic moms highly emotionally invested in perpetuating their false face. Keeping the false face frontward makes a narcissistic mother appear to be kind, compassionate, and empathetic. Her children will always be a means of gratifying and escalating this false self.

VULNERABLE NARCISSISM

Vulnerable narcissism is the other type. These narcissists are also known as fragile, compensatory, self-effacing, or closet narcissists. They have the same characteristics as a grandiose narcissist, except they would rather stay behind the scenes instead of being in the spotlight.

Because they prefer to stay away from attention, they're harder to recognize. They can go a long time before being discovered to be a narcissist. They're often quiet, shy, or reserved, but they're still emotionally demanding and draining for others to be around. Like grandiose narcissists, they feel entitled, but they're also insecure. They can be generous with their time or money as a way of getting compliments, affirmation, or praise, but because of their self-doubt, they would rather associate with people whom they idealize. They choose to attach to talented, famous, or influential individuals to satisfy their need to feel special.

Like grandiose narcissists, vulnerable narcissists believe they're faultless, and they get irritated when others fail to see their perfection. Their lives revolve around the task of convincing everyone of their greatness. They often present themselves as victims, regardless of the circumstances. They enjoy playing the victim role (I call it being a "poor me") to get attention in the form of sympathy or pity.

Vulnerable narcissists are prone to depression, mainly because they think that their life doesn't align with their ideas of what it should be or what they're entitled to. This inconsistency may cause them to act impulsively without considering the consequences. For example, they may abruptly quit their job before finding another because the work or their coworkers or supervisors don't match their expectations or fantasies.

Two Ways Of Getting Supply

Narcissism "subtypes" describe the *method* that grandiose or vulnerable narcissists use to get their emotional and egotistical needs met, known as "narcissistic supply." If the way of getting their narcissistic supply is easy to spot, the individual is probably an overt narcissist.

Overt Narcissism

While all narcissists will brag, take advantage of people, and speak negatively about others to make themselves look superior, *overt* narcissists will do these things in distinct, very noticeable ways. For example, overt narcissists attract attention to themselves directly in ways such as over-dressing, or dressing provocatively, talking too loudly, wearing attention-getting makeup, hairstyles, or accessories, or driving conspicuous vehicles. They require admiration, and if they don't get it, they react with rage, ridicule, mockery, or humiliation. They like to use charm and flattery so people will like them although they're arrogant, proud, and view others as insignificant or as competitors to conquer. They feel entitled and expect special treatment.

Covert Narcissism

Covert narcissism, on the other hand, is subtle, and it can be tricky to identify. Covert narcissists are more cautious and reserved in the ways they get their supply.

If we find ourselves denying, minimizing, or making excuses for someone's behavior, that's a red flag. If you start feeling like a detective on the lookout for reasons to explain someone's behavior, pay attention to that. They could be a covert narcissist.

Because of the reserved way that covert narcissists get their supply, it's understandable that covert narcissistic moms get their supply mainly from their children. It's about how her children make her appear as a mother. Whatever you do to make her look good in front of others is a form of supply for her. If you give her a gift, she'll brag about it because receiving a gift from her child makes her appear to be a well-loved mother. When she gives you gifts, though, there are always "strings" attached. She can't give for the sake of giving. She expects something in return, in the form of loyalty, emotional caretaking, secret-keeping, or admiration.

Taking care of her needs will be number one on her priority list, and her children's needs will be further down. If you question her, she'll assume you're challenging her, and she'll become defensive, maybe violent. She doesn't respect your boundaries or your privacy. She's totally at ease going into your personal space, looking in your purse, reading your diary, listening to your phone conversations, reading private mail and documents, and sharing your personal and private information with others. Because of this, you'll feel a sense of shame in multiple areas, but you won't realize that these behaviors are its source.

I spend a lot of time talking about covert narcissism because my mom is covert, and it's the subtype I'm most familiar with.

LIVING WITH A COVERT NARCISSISTIC MOTHER

If your mom is a covert narcissist, you may sense that something isn't "right" in your relationship, but you can't quite "put your finger on it." It could be the way she expresses herself, or that things she does or says confuse you. Sensing that something's not adding up, but not being able to identify what it is can stir up feelings of anxiety and the desire to avoid her. If your mom is a narcissist, it can feel like she's sucking the life right out of us; we may feel exhausted after spending time with her, and we don't understand the reasons *why*.

"Regardless of how anyone treats you, you stand to benefit. While some people teach you who you do want to be, others teach you who you don't want to be. And it's the people who teach you who you don't want to be that provide some of the most lasting and memorable lessons on social graces, human dignity, and the importance of acting with integrity."

—Kari Kampakis

As kids, if mom is a covert narcissist, we can't exactly avoid her, so we're likely to become hyperaware of her moods and behaviors instead. Our intuition, our gut feelings, alert us when something's going on that we don't comprehend. We know we need to be careful, and we may be sensing danger.

If your mother is a covert narcissist, your sense of self-preservation will more than likely intensify over time, causing you to become exceptionally alert and aware of your mother's behavior. You might have ongoing feelings of uneasiness when you're with her; it may feel like you're not entirely emotionally or physically safe. Those of us who are children of covert narcissists may have started feeling distrustful of our mothers without having a concrete reason, and this can make us question our judgment. That's the last thing we should do!

If there is no professional diagnosis, it doesn't mean we imagine the problem or that something's wrong with our perception. We're sensing something that we can't physically see or explain, but it's still authentic. Our intuition is real. When it alerts us, we need to pay attention.

Covert narcissist traits make it difficult for others to see anything "wrong" with mom. Most of the time, there's nothing concrete to point to. Sure, we have lots of examples of her strange and confusing behavior, and we can speak at length about her unusual way of thinking, perceiving, or expressing herself, including that she's either the victim or the hero in any scenario. Without a broader context or the experience of living with her, it's difficult for others to see that there's something fundamentally inappropriate going on. The biggest reasons for going undetected as a narcissist, I think, are the use of the false public self combined with subtle forms of manipulation and mind games like gaslighting and triangulation. All of these make it very hard for others, who only see her false face, to recognize her as a narcissist.

TRIANGULATION

A covert narcissist mother tends to sulk and employ passive-aggressive behavior: for example, giving backhanded compliments, using procrastination and withdrawal to avoid interaction or activity, and refusing to talk (Cherry 2019). They enjoy guilt-tripping and pushing responsibilities on us that aren't ours. They also like causing conflict between us and others. She uses a manipulative tactic called "triangulation": when one person manipulates the relationship between two other people by controlling the amount and type of communication they have. She controls the narrative, which generates rivalry between the two parties and acts as a way to "divide and conquer," playing one person against the other. My mother thoroughly enjoyed this game. She did it with me as well as cousins, aunts, and friends. A therapist once called it "stirring the pot," and I've held onto that analogy.

Triangulation is toxic, but you can learn to use techniques and tools to deal with it in a whole new and healthy way. For instance, you can start speaking directly to the other person in the triangle to remove your mother's input. Get your information directly rather than from your mother and suggest that others do the same. At the time I learned how to handle triangulation, I was decisively starting to take my personal power *back*. I was no longer willing to accept lies or gaslighting, and I started speaking up for myself. That was the beginning of my recovery. It's called "setting boundaries," and I write more about that in later chapters.

EXCLUSION

A covert narcissist-mom also likes to use "exclusionary behaviors," such as withholding affection and attention from us or temporarily withdrawing from our lives. Then she'll shower a specific person with copious amounts of love and attention. When she does this, it can feel like a punch in the gut, like she's punishing us. That's because it's exactly what she's doing, and it's deliberate. It gives her a rush of power and superiority.

She has no empathy and can't understand how we feel, but she knows that at that moment, she's in control and has the power to hurt us. When you feel excluded, it can become a great time to practice getting in touch with your emotions by becoming self-aware and practicing mindfulness. Validate yourself by acknowledging how her behavior makes you feel. Do you notice any patterns when she's about to make you feel like an outsider? Is there a way to halt those patterns before they start? If not, then practice getting comfortable with being an outsider. When you're excluded, practice controlling your emotions and recognizing your triggers. Think of your triggers as little suitcases that you need to unpack and examine the contents. You'll be surprised at what you find.

When you're ready, you'll begin to apply a bit of loving detachment and set some boundaries around the exclusionary behavior. (You'll learn more about detachment and boundary-setting in later chapters.)

GUILT

Narcissists don't feel a sense of remorse or conscience. They believe that everything they do is justified or is someone else's fault. They don't take responsibility for their actions, which makes them unable to feel guilt. To feel guilty, it's necessary to feel empathy and remorse.

Guilt is a positive and healthy thing. It's a form of cognitive dissonance, a way of holding a mirror up and seeing the discrepancy between "this is who you *say* you are, but this is what you *did*." We feel guilty when *"who we are"* and *"what we did"* are not aligned. This misalignment causes us to feel guilt and empathy for the person we wronged. For example, if I believe I'm a gentle, kind, and loving person, and I make a cruel remark to someone, my perception of "who I am" no longer matches my behavior: "what I did." A gentle, kind, and loving person would not intentionally say mean things. I would be motivated by feelings of guilt to apologize for my conduct. The cognitive dissonance that guilt provides drives us to atone for our inappropriate actions.

Feeling guilty, remorseful, or apologetic are beyond a narcissist's capabilities. We will never get an apology from a narcissist-mom. Instead, we'll get a weird version of an excuse where she justifies or defends what she did if she's even willing to admit what she did. Or we may get the silent treatment until she feels she's punished us sufficiently.

It's all so arbitrary, and somehow the message will always be that her actions were *our* fault.

With a covert narcissist-mom, her needs and emotions always come first, because they're of utmost importance to her. Her children's needs and feelings may or may not be relevant, depending on how she feels at the moment (about herself, about life, etc.). She sees everything as a competition, and nothing that has ever happened or will happen to her children could ever compare to what she has experienced. Her experiences are always more highly valued. This is known as "one-upmanship."

When we're around her, we'll eventually develop an apprehension of saying or doing the wrong thing, and a feeling of "walking on eggshells" or tippy-toeing around her to avoid upsetting her, making her angry, or setting her off. We live with a genuine understanding that we're not emotionally safe with her. She hijacks everything we say or do and makes it about herself. Anything we say or do that displeases her will be remembered, brought up, and held against us in the future, and so we try to avoid confrontation of any kind.

The result of this focus is that we start to feel responsible for her feelings and actions. We become her emotional guardians and caretakers even to the point that we allow her to isolate us from friends and family or to control whom we interact with.

We all need someone to talk to and share our problems with or bounce ideas off. Sharing with friends or family who aren't familiar with toxic relationships, and specifically narcissism, can frustrate or hurt us even more. Others don't know that they're invalidating us or discounting our experiences. They only know our mother's false face. That's why I repeatedly suggest talking to a neutral party, like a counselor who understands this disorder.

Mixed Messages

If your mother is a covert narcissist, you might notice discrepancies between her words and her actions, meaning that they don't match up. This can make you feel edgy (that "walking on eggshells" feeling), and being in this state of mind heightens your *fight-or-flight* response. The fight-or-flight mode causes a sudden and quick hormone release that activates the body's ability to deal with danger or threats. Adrenaline and noradrenaline are two of the hormones released during the fight-or-flight response; they increase blood pressure, heart, and breathing rate. We'll talk more about the fight-or-flight response and what it does in later chapters. In the meantime, just know that mixed messages contribute to feelings of being on high-alert, edginess, and confusion.

A narcissistic mom's mixed messages are a type of communication where one party sends conflicting information to another, either verbally or nonverbally.

Mixed messages come in various packages:

- What she says conflicts with what she previously said.

- What she does conflicts with what she previously did.

- What she says conflicts with what she does.

- What she says conflicts with her facial expressions or body language.

An example of "words not matching facial expression/body language" would be when mom says she's happy to see you, but she frowns, and her tone of voice is sarcastic. This would be confusing because of the conflicting information you're getting: "happy" means that a person's face would show joy, usually by smiling. A happy person would not frown. "Sarcasm" is used to mock or convey contempt. It's used to inflict pain and is often described as wounding.

Do you see how these mixed messages can cause feelings of confusion? In this example, an empowering response would be: "I'm confused. You say you're happy to see me, yet you look so _____ (angry, sad, depressed, etc.) I don't get it. What's going on?" This response puts the confusion back on her. It informs her that you're aware of what she's doing, and it sets the expectation for her to clarify her communication. It signals that you're not going to tolerate that kind of behavior any longer. It's empowering because you don't have to accept the confusion or ruminate over it anymore.

An example of "words not matching actions" would be when mom brags about how caring and empathetic she is, but you haven't seen any evidence of this. There's a term for this behavior; it's called *virtue signaling*. When a person indeed possesses a character trait, they don't have to announce or advertise it. They simply live it, and people notice. Covert narcissists want us to believe what they tell us about themselves, instead of what we see for ourselves. I view this as another form of gaslighting.

I'm very familiar with receiving mixed messages because my mom gave them on an almost daily basis. I was very young when I began to rely on my mom to tell me what was "real" and what wasn't, because of my state of constant confusion. I didn't know whether to believe her tone of voice, her facial expressions, her words, or her actions. I often didn't know what to believe, and I'd spend ridiculous amounts of time ruminating over confusing scenarios, trying to make sense of them. When I was a child, if I questioned my mother in an attempt at clarification and understanding, she would slap me across my face. She believed that children should not question adults.

As a result of living with mixed messages and other confusing behaviors, I was always "figuring it out," wondering, and creating explanations. I think you can see how this could contribute to feelings of self-doubt and a growing reliance upon my mother to interpret my reality for me. As I grew, I became mistrustful of my judgment and doubtful of my ability to remember accurately.

"Life can only be understood backwards, but it must be lived forwards."

—Søren Kierkegaard

INTRODUCING: BOUNDARIES

One therapist explained my mom's behavior to me by saying, "irrational behavior is, by definition, unexplainable." That statement was a revelation to me, as simple as it seems. I tended to relive my confusing experiences with her over and over and *over*. Usually, it was something she said or did that didn't make sense or confused me. I also ruminated on things that she later *denied* saying or doing even though I'd personally witnessed them. I wasted a lot of my life trying to explain her irrational behavior so that it would make some kind of sense to me. I did that because I needed the confusion to go away. Walking around confused, in fight-or-flight mode, focusing on her behavior, was no way to live, and I'd been doing it all of my life at that point.

I realized that I had to learn how to speak up for myself, to point out mixed messages and inconsistencies when they happened, to be emotionally strong enough to hold her accountable. I needed to learn how to insist upon clarification and set boundaries around these and other confusing and disturbing behaviors.

Boundaries protect us from someone else's behavior or from engaging in activities that we'd rather not. Setting healthy boundaries is a type of self-care: we get to determine what's acceptable to us and what's not. They help us to set limits that protect and empower us, and they pertain to "me" rather than to others. My boundaries are for me and are under my control. I base my limits on "what I need" to maintain my safety, emotional stability, and mental health. Setting boundaries isn't a way to control others. Boundaries aren't for changing another person's behavior. They're a way to have personal limits for ourselves. They're not emotional; they're factual.

After I began my healing journey in earnest, whenever my mother said or did anything that confused me, I reminded myself that she's afflicted with a type of mental disorder. The disorder caused her to behave irrationally, and irrational behavior has no explanation. I told myself that my time is valuable and that it's better spent focusing on and enjoying my life. These healthy and empowering thoughts were and are freeing; they're a form of self-awareness and of accepting reality. They're a way of "letting go" and *not* trying to control the outcome. I'll talk more about the topics of letting go, boundaries, and managing consequences later on.

If you "Google" narcissism, you'll find many more types and subtypes, that I haven't included in this book. They aren't recognized as "official" types or subtypes of NPD by the American Psychological Association in the DSM-5, and I wanted to stick with what the American Psychological Association, the recognized authority on mental illness, has to say.

I've researched other kinds of narcissism discussed on the web, for example, toxic, somatic, cerebral, exhibitionist, antisocial…far too many to name. To talk about and describe each of the combinations possible is beyond the scope of this book. I'm confident that these all exist in varying degrees on the narcissism spectrum and are diagnosable by a professional using the diagnostic criteria described earlier.

These numerous types seem to be varying combinations of the two recognized types and subtypes, only differing in their presentations and methods for obtaining the supply. Suffice it to say that each of them is possible and diagnosable by a professional using section III of the DSM-5 criteria.

This chapter was pretty heavy. Narcissism is a complicated disorder, not easily diagnosed. It takes a mental health professional who has a thorough understanding of mental illness, personality disorders, and narcissism in particular to diagnose it. And most narcissists won't get to the point of getting a professional diagnosis anyway.

"Your mother doesn't need a professional diagnosis for you to start making healthy changes for yourself."

If your relationship with your mother confuses you because you're getting mixed messages from her, if it feels like nothing you do is ever good enough, if you are tolerating cruelty, then your relationship isn't healthy.

A label or diagnosis doesn't matter. If you're unhappy, frustrated, or confused, labeling your mother isn't necessary for you to stop tolerating the mistreatment.

TAKEAWAYS

- There are two main types of narcissism: grandiose and vulnerable, and there are two subtypes: overt vs. covert.

- Acquaintances, friends, and extended family of a narcissist-mom often don't see the false face for what it is.

- Children of narcissists have a hard time getting people to understand or believe what's going on at home.

ACTION FOR HEALING

1. If you had/have a mother (caretaker/mother figure) who showed symptoms of narcissism, write about these symptoms. Talk about the possible type of narcissism it was and include its probable subtype. Give examples that support your thought process.

2. Write the insights or "aha" moments you had while reading this chapter.

3. Those of us who've discovered we've been negatively affected by our mother's narcissism often feel sad and experience symptoms of grief. Write about how you feel concerning the effects your mother's narcissism has had on you.

4. Have you experienced triangulation? Write about it. Who was in the triangle? How did you handle it? What will be different about the way you handle it next time?

5. Have you experienced being excluded by your mother? Write about that: where it happened, who was there, how it made you feel. Include how you'll deal with it the next time it happens.

Chapter Five
THE TRAUMATIZED BRAIN

"There are wounds that never show on the body that are deeper and more hurtful than anything that bleeds."

—Laurell K. Hamilton, *Mistral's Kiss*

I remember a time when I was about six years old on a Saturday morning. Still sleepy and bleary-eyed, I walked into the kitchen where my mother was standing, holding my toddler sibling. Chubby little arms reached toward the table, fingers opening and closing; the little one urged: "Me 'nut! Me uh-nut!" and in an instant that still boggles my mind, my mother whirled around and mightily backhanded my face, shouting, "*Who* told about the donuts?? WHO TOLD ABOUT THE GODDAMN DONUTS?"

And in a nano-second, I was flooded with feelings of shock, fear, confusion, physical pain, humiliation, shame. And *anger.*

You see, I had no idea that there were donuts. I tried explaining that to my mother through tearful sobs, but she refused to listen, utterly convinced of my guilt. She snarled through bared teeth that I was a *liar* and screamed in my face to "GET TO YOUR ROOM" so ferociously that I ran.

Her face was purplish-red, and her eyes bulged in a way that, to a six-year-old, made her look vicious. I ran to my room, absolutely terrified.

I was completely baffled by the instantaneous chaos and trauma. I'd been truthful. What had happened? What had I walked into? What had I done wrong? I kept going over and over (and over) those few minutes between waking up and going to the kitchen. I wanted so desperately to explain and understand what happened, mostly so I could make sure that it would never happen again. I was already feeling responsible for her rages and codependent at age six.

I fell asleep weeping, feeling rejected, unloved, unwanted, defeated, completely confused, frustrated, misunderstood, and with no justification for my punishment. To top it off, I felt guilty for whatever it was I'd done to deserve the punishment. I was completely ignored for the rest of the morning, in my room, a form of the "Silent Treatment." And even so, I *continued* to try to figure out how **I** had caused this incident. Seriously. I tried to figure that out.

Later that day, my cousin reminded my mother, who'd forgotten, that the baby had spent time with them together the previous evening. While they ate donuts.

I was vindicated and grateful. I don't think my mother would've ever believed me. I would've continued trying to convince her of my blamelessness until I eventually accepted defeat. I would've accepted her version of the story; that it was me who revealed the donuts' presence, and that I just couldn't *remember* doing it. In effect, I would've accepted the gaslighting as I had so many times before.

As I matured, I often went through lengthy explanations to clarify and justify myself to others whenever I'd made a decision or took action. I also felt the need to document those by taking pictures, keeping notes, or making copies of texts and emails. I felt a strong need to "cover my back." One never knows when they'll have to *prove* that they did or didn't do something, right?

Thanks to recovery work, I no longer feel the need to justify. Yay for me! And if I make a statement, I no longer feel the need to prove its truthfulness or validity, and I'm good with that.

WHAT TRAUMA DOES

To fully understand how neglectful or traumatic experiences affect human beings, we need to understand some things about our brains.

The key player is the limbic system, which is an intricate network of structures located in the brain beneath the cerebral cortex (the brain's outer layer of folded gray matter, which plays a vital role in consciousness). Consisting of four main parts—the hypothalamus, the amygdala, the thalamus, and the hippocampus—this system controls basic emotions such as fear, pleasure, and anger. It's involved with instinct, mood, motivation, and emotional behavior. Regarding trauma, I'll focus on the hippocampus and the amygdala because of their roles in memory and emotional response.

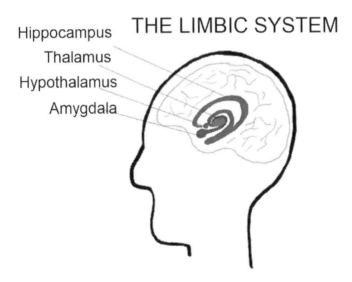

THE LIMBIC SYSTEM

Hippocampus
Thalamus
Hypothalamus
Amygdala

CREATING MEMORIES: THE AMYGDALA AND HIPPOCAMPUS

We have two amygdalae, one on each side of our brains, often called the "emotional brain" because it's involved with our emotional responses to memories.

The amygdala's job is to convert and move information out of short-term into long-term memory and connect emotions to those memories (Krause-Utz et al. 2017).

Whenever we experience any traumatic episode, a hormone called adrenaline is released from our adrenal glands, located just above our kidneys. This release of adrenaline causes a memory of the trauma to be created in the amygdala. This memory is not stored linearly like a story. Instead, it's saved according to how our five senses experienced the trauma as it happened. So, the traumatic memories are stored as bits of visual images, smells, sounds, tastes, or physical contact. The amygdala then gives meaning, as well as a particular degree of emotional intensity, to the traumatic event.

If the amygdala is continually on high alert from real or perceived threats, emotions won't become self-regulated like they're supposed to. When our emotions aren't self-regulated, we will respond to old, buried memories with an automatic, knee-jerk behavior called "triggering." Triggering is caused when the brain can no longer distinguish between something that's a real threat and something that's not. When we're triggered, the amygdala misinterprets input from our senses, eyes, ears, nose, mouth, or skin, as being dangerous or threatening, even when it's not.

And if we continually live in this high-alert, fight-or-flight survival mode, we'll likely begin coping in ways that aren't good for us. We may lie, depend on drugs, overeat, steal, or basically do whatever it takes to help us cope with the unmanageable stress.

Another essential structure in the limbic system that's related to how we handle trauma and stress is the horseshoe-shaped hippocampus.

The hippocampus also moves information from short-term to long-term memory, but its main job is cataloging memories for storage and retrieval, and developing new memories about past experiences.

The hippocampus is in charge of remembering locations for objects and people. When we remember that we left our keys on the kitchen counter, we're using our hippocampus. We use the hippocampus for spatial memory, navigating, and orientation. Without it, we wouldn't remember where the kitchen counter is or how to get there from where we are in relation. This is critical information about our surroundings, and we rely on it to find our way around.

The hippocampus continues to be the focus of research regarding cognition (understanding through thought, experience, and senses) and memory-retention in post-traumatic stress disorder (PTSD) (Kolassa and Elbert 2007). You'll learn more about PTSD in later chapters.

TAKEAWAYS

- The amygdala's job is to convert and move information from short term to long-term memory and to connect emotions to these memories. The amygdala gives meaning and a degree of emotional intensity to the memory.

- The hippocampus continues to be the focus of research regarding cognition (understanding through thought, experience, and senses) and memory-retention in post-traumatic stress disorder (PTSD).

- Traumatic memories are stored as bits of visual images, smells, sounds, tastes, or physical contact.

- When emotions aren't self-regulated, we continue to respond to old, buried memories with an automatic, knee-jerk behavior called "triggering."

ACTION FOR HEALING

1. Acknowledge your traumatic memories. In as much detail as you care to, create a section in your journal just for these memories and add to them as you remember them. Include those experiences that still leave you feeling hurt or confused today.

2. Acknowledge your triggers. What are they? As you work through this book and continue your healing process afterward, make it a priority to become aware of your triggers. Make a

section in your journal specifically for your triggers and list them there as you discover them.

3. Include your thoughts about where each trigger came from and how you handle each of them currently.

4. Give a recent example of a reaction to one of your triggers. Think about ways you can respond differently the next time this trigger comes up.

Chapter Six
LOOKING BACK: OUR PAST

"The conflict between the will to deny horrible events and the will to proclaim them aloud is the central dialectic of psychological trauma."

—Judith Lewis Herman, *Trauma and Recovery: The Aftermath of Violence—From Domestic Abuse to Political Terror*

NOT GOOD ENOUGH

Those of us who grew up with a mother who parented by blaming, shaming, humiliating, intimidating, manipulating, mocking, using sarcasm, or lying, likely felt confused, socially awkward, "less than," and probably not "good enough." Growing up in a narcissistic family meant that we repeatedly and consistently got the message that everybody else's needs, especially our mothers, were more important than our own.

When we carry these beliefs into adulthood, we can easily become action-takers and "fixers," always attempting to control outcomes and figure out other people's problems. We take responsibilities that aren't ours, and we may even get a lot of satisfaction from acquiring such "projects"—always helping, forever putting our own needs and desires last, if we acknowledge them at all. We feel unloved and resentful, but we don't understand why.

Growing up in this kind of oppressive environment most likely meant we couldn't freely express our feelings or ask questions because either our mother wasn't interested in them, or it didn't feel safe to do so. When we become adults, it's harder for us to talk about personal things or have difficult discussions, and we avoid conflict at all costs.

If we begin believing that we're fundamentally flawed or undeserving of kindness and love as children, we may willingly but unintentionally become the dumping ground for other's emotional garbage as adults. Though we don't like it, we might unconsciously believe we don't deserve anything better than the kind of treatment we endured as kids.

"Growing up in a toxic or neglectful environment can create problems that can last a lifetime."

THE IMPORTANCE OF VALIDATION

Validation is the act of recognizing or affirming someone's feelings or thoughts as sound or worthwhile. The act of validating is an essential aspect of parenting because it opens the door for safe communication. Feeling heard and understood allows people to trust, which is a cornerstone of every relationship, especially between mothers and their children.

A validating mother listens to what her child is saying. She understands that her child has their own emotions and thoughts, even if she doesn't necessarily agree with them. Validation is a nonjudgmental and supportive action that requires empathy.

When a child falls and skins her knee, a validating mother will understand that the crying child is in pain and requires some form of caretaking or soothing to feel better. The remedy could simply be a verbal expression of empathy and understanding, (acknowledging that the child is hurting), or hugging and kissing her, or applying an antibiotic and a Band-Aid. The point is that this child knows she's been heard, understood, cared for, and loved. She feels worthy of mom's time and effort and believes she's valued. This is *validation*. The mother may not think the injury is as severe as the child may believe, but she doesn't judge. She accepts how the child feels; she doesn't minimize or negate her child's feelings.

A validating mother would say something like, "Wow! You're really crying hard! Your knee must hurt a lot. Let's see if I can make you feel better."

In 2016, an observational study was done to see if a relationship existed between a mother's emotional validation and the degree of awareness her child has about their own emotions. They found that the mother's degree of emotional validation and invalidation were accurate predictors of the child's perception of their emotional state. These results suggest that children's attention to their emotional states may be formed by their mother's use of emotional validation and invalidation (Lambie and Lindberg 2016).

If our mother doesn't "see us" and validate us as individuals who have thoughts, feelings, and goals of our own, we may start thinking, feeling, or believing that we don't matter. If we establish this mindset as children, that we're not good enough, or that it's OK to be mistreated or unloved or ignored, then we won't learn how to validate ourselves. We won't know how to comfortably acknowledge our positive characteristics or our personal or professional accomplishments, either.

Of course, we may receive validation from other people besides our mothers. Caring adults, older siblings, or a father can affirm and support us too. But being approved of and understood by our mother is a unique and vital experience.

"Because validation requires empathy, a narcissistic mother will not be able to perform this responsibility."

As I mentioned before, if we haven't experienced what it's like to be treated as unique beings who matter, we may form the belief that others' needs are more important than our own. This is an important idea to note because *a belief is created when our feelings become connected with our thoughts* (Lamia 2012). Thank you, amygdala.

Without examining our original childhood beliefs, we may simply bring them along with us into adulthood, even though they're no longer relevant, are self-limiting, and untrue.

When I was four years old, I was alone outside, barefoot, and stubbed my bare big toe; it bled, and my little self knew it was the worst pain I'd ever experienced. I was appalled by the hanging flap of skin, and I was afraid.

On this particular day, my mother, in response to my limping into the house, wailing and interrupting her TV show, angrily grabbed my forearm and hauled me into the bathroom. She proceeded to run water over my foot, adding a whole new dimension of pain. The entire time, she furiously and loudly berated and humiliated me for running (I wasn't running), "not looking where you're going," and for not knowing how to walk without hurting myself. I'd dared to lack the focus and navigational skill required and had burdened her with my injury.

There was no kiss, no hug, no feeling of being understood or valued, cared for, or even loved. There was no Band-Aid. Just continuous berating and humiliating, which ended with an admonishment to be more careful next time and not let it happen again. I was sent back outside, feeling ashamed of myself and embarrassed by my inability to negotiate the walkway safely. I rejected others' empathy or sympathy for my injury and redirected their attention to anything other than myself. I didn't feel worthy of anyone's concern or kindness.

To this day, remembering this event confounds me. Over the years, I've explained it to myself in various ways. But the explanation that rings most true is that this must have been a narcissistic injury for my mother. A narcissistic injury is anything that threatens the 'false self.' Her rage at me for falling made no sense, and she flipped the scenario to make herself the victim: because of me, she had to get off her chair, miss a portion of her TV show (those days were before "pause, rewind and fast forward" TV programming or DVR), and treat my wound. She was angry because I "should have known better" than to cause her this inconvenience.

When I became a mother, I was incredibly aware that I wanted to raise my children very differently than I had been. I knew that I sorely lacked healthy parenting skills and parent role-models. I wanted to learn how to parent lovingly and responsibly. I needed to learn proper parenting techniques, and I tried to find healthy mother role models to imitate. I was on the lookout for them everywhere I went.

I remember sitting on my porch when my neighbor's young child fell and hurt herself. The child's mother ran over and scooped her up, sat her on a step, and examined her bleeding knee. I watched them very carefully. I saw the mother gently blow on the knee, probably to minimize the sting. I later learned from the mom that she applied antiseptic, administered a chewable pain killer, and applied a cheerful Band-Aid. The little girl was outside playing again in a matter of minutes. That mom was a validating mother. She affirmed her child in a kind and loving manner, and that was the kind of mother I wanted to be.

Here's my point: If we don't learn that we're unique beings who *matter* simply because we exist, and if we don't know how to identify our emotions because we've never learned how, we're at risk for developing unhealthy coping mechanisms. We may have a hard time accepting when someone likes or tries to befriend us, and we question why they would want to. If someone does something kind for us, we may assume it's a form of manipulation, or we may be confused by it. When our emotional, psychological, or physical needs go unmet, we often find other possibly harmful or maladaptive ways to get by.

PERSONAL LIMITS

When we grow up in an oppressive or toxic environment, we don't know that there are ways to protect ourselves from mistreatment. We may grow up to unconsciously broadcast the message that we exist to be of service to others and that it doesn't matter how they treat us. As adults, we may accept disrespect, unfair or unkind treatment, and even physical, verbal, and emotional abuse.

If we haven't seen healthy boundaries modeled, then we don't know what a healthy boundary is or how to create one, so we become hypervigilant instead. This means that our amygdala has stored the threatening behavior patterns in our memory for our self-preservation, and our focus becomes external, focusing on others' behavior and moods. We're continually on guard, ready for, or preparing for danger. This is the fight-or-flight mode mentioned previously, and it contributes heavily to C-PTSD, an anxiety disorder caused by exposure to traumatic events.

This preoccupation with focusing on others also contributes to becoming codependent.

INTRODUCING: CODEPENDENCE

When we have low self-worth, it's natural to feel that we're not worthy or good enough to ask for what we want or need. Instead, we learn to manipulate people and consequences to get our needs met. We may discover that we seemingly have no choice but to take on responsibilities that aren't ours. As we mature, in order for us to feel emotionally or physically safe, it can feel necessary to control as much of our environment as we can. We do this in an attempt to avoid nasty surprises. Feeling like we're in control makes us feel safe. We begin managing aspects of others' lives, and we may even believe that we're emotionally stronger, more capable, and better at it than they are. When we spend more time taking care of or focusing on our mom and others, or when we try to control them or the outcomes of their behavior, we have become codependent.

> *"When we're raised by people who cannot, or refuse to, "see us," don't affirm or value us, or mistreat us, we may begin to believe we're unworthy of the positive things in life; like love, affection, joy, success and peace."*

Codependency develops as a self-protective response. It's a way of coping with a stressful or unhealthy, traumatic, or abusive environment and can be learned by watching and imitating other codependents. It's a learned behavior that can be passed down through generations.

As we've seen, codependents willingly play by others' "rules," and in doing so, lose their own identity. It's an emotional and behavioral illness that affects a person's ability to have healthy, mutually satisfying relationships in adulthood.

If we're codependent, we most likely believe that we know what's best for other people and their lives, and we think we know how to fix their problems. We want them to follow our unsolicited advice and are often hurt or angered when they don't.

To a codependent, helping and fixing other people or their problems feels good. They feel needed and are highly attracted to people who could use their help. Codependents enjoy offering suggestions and advice even though they haven't been asked for them. If we're codependent, we feel responsible for people and issues that aren't our responsibility, and if we don't attempt to help, fix, or control, we often feel guilty or ashamed. It feels wrong not to jump in, take charge, or aid others who seem to be struggling, even though they haven't reached out for assistance. We just feel that somehow, it's our job to take action, take over, and fix.

If we're codependent, we most likely don't have boundaries. We'll disclose almost everything we think and do, and we'll assume that we won't be believed. We'll overexplain our choices and behavior because if we've not enjoyed our mother's validation (or if we've been continually invalidated), we still crave to be heard, understood, and affirmed. We'll continuously seek affirmation outside of ourselves to feel "good enough" or that we matter. Doing this is called obtaining "external validation," and codependents seek external validation and affirmation any way they can get it. It's often described as being needy, "clingy," or insecure.

Codependents continually look for someone to please. When we're codependent, we feel the need to make excuses for other's mistreatment of us or their poor behavior in general. We explain to ourselves why they're abusing us and why it's OK for them to do so. We often take the blame. We minimize and deny the pain they cause. Codependents are famously known for their discomfort with saying "no."

Healthy coping mechanisms, on the other hand, help us to make sense of confusing or threatening life experiences and to respond appropriately in wholesome ways. You've heard the saying "when life gives you lemons, make lemonade"? Well, that's a coping skill: taking something negative and turning it into a positive. In reality, nothing has actually changed. Life has still given us lemons, but instead of getting angry, depressed, or feeling slighted or misunderstood, we choose to look at it another way. When we use healthy coping, we're able to reframe adverse events in a way that feels better.

INTRODUCING: DISSOCIATION

"Dissociation" is another coping mechanism, defined as losing the sense of who we are, where we are, or what we're doing. When the body and brain haven't formed the necessary connection that allows a healthy sense of self to develop, dissociation is the result (Eddy 2018). This can also be a protective response because it provides an emotional separation from trauma or abuse as it's happening. It's sometimes compared to having an "out-of-body" experience as if watching a movie rather than experiencing trauma or abuse firsthand (Hartney 2019).

One of the keys to healing from toxicity and developing healthy coping skills is to acknowledge our codependency and to begin recovering from it. We must learn how to change our perceptions as well as our responses. Healing also requires us to examine childhood beliefs from an adult perspective and release those that don't serve us, to replace them with new ones that do. We have to accept that we can't fix or heal other people. We only have control of ourselves, our attitudes, and our choices. To heal, we need to focus on ourselves.

Takeaways

- Growing up in a toxic or neglectful environment can create problems that can last a lifetime.

- Childhood trauma physically changes the brain and negatively impacts the way it functions.

- If we begin believing that we're fundamentally flawed or undeserving of kindness and love, we may willingly, but unintentionally, become the dumping ground for other's emotional garbage as adults.

- The act of validating is an essential aspect of parenting because it establishes a feeling of safety.

- Trust is a cornerstone of every relationship, especially between mothers and their children.

- Validation requires empathy; therefore, a narcissistic mother will not be able to perform this responsibility.

- Codependents gradually lose their identity.

- One of the keys to healing from toxicity and developing healthy coping skills is to acknowledge our codependency and to begin to recover from it.

Action for Healing

1. Think of ways that your mother validated you while you were growing up. Did she listen when you spoke? Did she

acknowledge how you felt? Did she dismiss you or tell you that you shouldn't feel the way you did? Did she accept your memories "as is," or did she want you to remember certain events differently? Create a section for validation in your journal and write in detail about these.

2. Do you like to "help" and "fix" other people or their problems? Give recent examples of ways that you've helped others or tried to fix them or their problems. Did they ask for this help? Did you jump in and get involved because you knew what to do? Did they accept your help? How did they respond? How did this make you feel? What did you think about the outcome? What have you learned? Write about how you felt in this scenario and what you can do differently next time.

Chapter Seven
NARCISSISM AWARENESS GRIEF

*"Whatever the situation may be, in order to fully achieve peace within yourself,
it is necessary for those who have been victims of narcissistic personalities to
complete all the stages of acceptance and learn to grow beyond
their previously fabricated reality."*

—Christine Hammond

So what's next? If you've been affected by your mother's narcissism, are you stuck living with the toxic effects? The answer is no, absolutely not! You can do recovery work and move forward into a healthier mindset and life. You can learn to set healthy boundaries to feel safe and secure, and you can lose the need to be in control of people and outcomes, and begin prioritizing yourself without feeling guilty about it.

"Narcissism awareness grief" (NAG) is a real thing, and a term coined by Dr. Christine Hammond.

I remember very clearly what it was like to experience NAG. As I slowly became aware of the effects my mother's narcissism had on me, I felt a mixture of shock, denial, disbelief, and a sense of overwhelming sadness that kept me focused on my childhood and the resentment that I felt. To begin the healing process, I knew I needed to process each stage of my grief and finally move into acceptance. Doing this takes time. To fully recover, you must be willing to give yourself unlimited, unpressured time, allowing each step to unfold at its own pace.

In my early years of therapy, before NAG (narcissism awareness grief) and before I even knew what exactly I needed to recover from, I focused on dealing with low self-confidence and self-esteem. I was always second-guessing myself, and I had a myriad of codependency symptoms. My therapist suggested that I "presented" much like an "adult child of an alcoholic" (ACA).

Adultchildren.org posts a list of personality traits that many ACA's have in common. These traits are known as the "laundry list"; a combination of C-PTSD and codependency symptoms. The list includes isolation, fear of authority figures, approval-seeking, lost identity, frightened by angry people, an overdeveloped sense of responsibility, being concerned with others rather than self, feeling guilty for protecting ourselves (setting boundaries), and confusing love with pity.

There was no substance abuse in my family of origin, yet I related to many laundry list items. At that time, maternal narcissism was virtually unheard of, so we agreed that my treatment approach would be that of an ACA.

Mental health professionals now know and understand that the word "dysfunctional" applies to other kinds of families besides those affected by alcoholism. For example, the Adult Children of Alcoholics® informational website, adultchildren.org, includes "dysfunctional families" in their target audience. The laundry list applies to them, as well.

During my course of therapy as an ACA, I was encouraged to read the research done in the late 1970s by Dr. Claudia Black, Ph.D. Her line of inquiry involved how children are affected by a parent's substance abuse. It was she who started the "adult child" movement and who identified the rules of dysfunctional families: "Don't Talk, Don't Trust, Don't Feel." I discovered that, much like my childhood environment, ACAs grew up in unpredictable, often chaotic environments. Inconsistency, irregularity, lack of supervision and boundaries, and little to no parental involvement are the norm in an alcoholic home, just as they had been in my own. It seemed it was true that ACAs and I were preoccupied with our parent's irrational behavior. We felt like we were always in fight-or-flight survival mode. We frequently took our parent's "emotional temperature" and adjusted our moods and conduct accordingly.

Because they were so busy emotionally and sometimes physically taking care of their alcoholic parent, ACA's emotional needs went unmet, just as mine had. As adults, we all had difficulty identifying our feelings and caring for ourselves. It was an astounding discovery for me to learn that other kids grew up in households much like my own and that we shared some of the same challenges as adults, seemingly related to our upbringings.

At some point during those years, when I was actively pursuing healing and personal growth, a therapist presented the idea that my mother likely had an undiagnosed and untreated mental illness, probably a personality disorder. Hearing this news was exciting and validating for me because I had suspected as much for a very long time.

As I came to grasp the impact that my mother's mental illness had on me, I felt a gamut of emotions—denial, sadness, rage, and everything in-between and back.

THERE'S A NAME FOR IT

If there's a pattern of ongoing power struggles, manipulation, gaslighting, or cruelty with your mother, and it causes you to doubt your memory, judgment, or sanity, your relationship is harmful to you. The best course of action is to accept that you cannot change or control her behavior; you can only control your own. When you fully understand and accept this, the ball is truly in your court. The next moves are up to you.

You see, when we discover that the traumatic lifestyle we've endured as children has an actual name, it's a massive relief at first. There's an initial rush of validation, and we suddenly realize that we're not alone, that we're not crazy, and that we haven't imagined any of it. Narcissistic trauma and abuse are real things, and we can recover from it.

"Your mother doesn't need a diagnosis for you to determine that your relationship with her is unhealthy."

For those of you who are beginning to, or have recently, become aware that your mother's perspective is her problem, not any shortcoming in yourself, you're likely feeing a colossal torrent of conflicting emotions, and you may not understand why. As you begin to accept this new way of perceiving and understanding your mother, you may begin to understand that your mother's perspective is dysfunctional. There is nothing—and there never was—anything inherently wrong with you, as you may have been led to believe.

NAG begins when we become aware of our mother's narcissism and realize the ways it impacted us.

The Six Stages of NAG

Much like the famous Kubler-Ross "five stages of grief," there are several stages of Narcissism Awareness Grief. They're not linear, so they're not experienced in any particular order. In fact, we can go back and forth between the stages throughout the process of grieving. But every step must be experienced before we can get to the final stage, which is "acceptance." It's also possible to become stuck in any phase for any length of time and never actually enter into acceptance.

"Staying vulnerable is a risk we have to take if we want to experience connection."

——Brené Brown

The difference between the two grief models is that NAG has an additional and essential phase called "rewriting." (Hammond 2019). This is where serious healing begins.

1. **Denial:** After reading, thinking, processing, and talking about maternal narcissism, you may begin to entertain the idea that your mother might be on the narcissism spectrum. This idea may be something you've never considered before. It may make you uncomfortable. Even if you're confident that she is affected, you might continue minimizing its' impact until you reach the point where you can't any longer. At that juncture, you'll begin to become aware of the scope of her illness and how it impacts the people in her life.

2. **Anger:** The anger that follows the growing awareness of your mother's narcissism can be intense. You may be angry with yourself for not seeing it before; you may be fuming with

previous therapists who did not see it. You may be furious with family members who encouraged you to listen to or believe your mom, and you might be furious with anyone who believed in your mother's false face. I think that what we're feeling in this stage is a kind of "righteous indignation," a natural response to anyone's mistreatment or abuse. If we witness injustices like someone being mistreated, bullied, or abused in any way, we naturally feel this kind of anger. This rage is hugely motivating for change.

3. **Bargaining:** You may wish your childhood was different. I remember wondering what my childhood would've been like if I'd had a mother who was able to truly love and care for me more than her image and what my adult life might've been like if I'd grown up feeling as if I mattered. You may have these kinds of thoughts too, or you might even shame yourself with thoughts like, "Why didn't I see this sooner?" or " I'm so stupid. I've wasted my life listening to and believing her." Many of your questions will have no real answer.

I cried a lot at first; in fact, any time I thought about the possibility that my mother is a narcissist. You may cry too or feel a profound sense of loss and sadness. Like me, you may feel robbed of your childhood and anger at the injustice of that happening to you. It's essential to see that, in this stage, you may be doing what your mother would do to you: insult, berate and question the validity of your thoughts and feelings. Be aware of that. Be kind to yourself. You actually need to go through this dark period of questioning so you'll be able to enter the rewriting phase later.

4. **Depression:** When I understood that I could not "help" my mother to change, or get her to see me differently, or change

her victim mentality, I became very, very sad. When it began to dawn on me that she would *never* change—that she was incapable of change—my sadness turned into depression. I'd formed a rudimentary understanding that I'd have to live with this new information from now on. I'd have to change the way I interacted and related to my mother for my protection. I saw that I had missed multiple unrecoverable opportunities in my life because I had adopted her limited and incorrect beliefs about me. I saw how my relationships, in fact, every aspect of my life, had been negatively impacted by her faulty ideas and opinions of me, which I had accepted and internalized. I worked on accepting the fact that there was nothing I could do to make my mother interested in me as a person or to receive me in my imperfection. I had to accept that she would continue to belittle, shame, and intimidate me and that she would never feel a bit of remorse, let alone apologize to me. She was going to remain manipulative, critical, blaming, and attention-seeking. It was a heavy feeling to recognize that I had a lot of work ahead of me, to reconcile the past, and to heal myself while my mother felt no accountability or responsibility.

5. **Rewriting:** This stage is exclusive to NAG, and it's where we can really do a lot of healing. It's about taking this new understanding of maternal narcissism and applying it to our past. When we begin to accept our mother's narcissism, we begin to understand how internalizing our mother's faulty perspective of us has negatively impacted us in our lives. So we must start to see things differently. We will form new ideas about ourselves. We will learn to think new thoughts like, "My mother was not capable of feeling maternal love because of her illness. It had nothing to do with me. I am and always have been lovable." And "My mother wasn't capable of feeling empathy. It wasn't that I didn't matter. I have always mattered."

I always mattered, but my mother couldn't see it or acknowledge it. I have flaws, and that's absolutely OK. Everybody does. There is no such thing as perfection, but my mother continues to chase this false ideal. Too bad for her. When we update our historical view of ourselves by using this new information about narcissism, we can transform. We can begin to see ourselves in a whole, new, and healthy light. For many of us, this is the beginning of discovering that we are likable, and that we like ourselves and that we matter. We may begin to prioritize self-care and set personal boundaries, quite possibly moving into the happiest time of our lives.

6. **Acceptance:** As we work our way through the stages, this last piece comes pretty effortlessly. We finally accept our mother's narcissism as the permanent disability it is. We see her narcissism as a revelation of sorts, and there's an exciting feeling of freedom when we understand that we don't have any responsibility, *or the ability*, to change her. We're finally able to let go of the effects of our dysfunctional childhood. We welcome the understanding that narcissists don't change, which makes them very predictable. Now we can anticipate our mother's behavior, and we can make interacting with her feel safer for us, or at least more tolerable. As our expectations change, we may experience a sense of peace we never thought possible. Now we can determine what kind and how much exposure we will subject ourselves to, and we can plan accordingly. Some of us may decide to have no contact at all, and some may choose to have limited contact with strict enforceable boundaries. For example, I decided to continue my relationship with my mother, but with limited contact. I had moved to another state when the opportunity had presented itself, and doing this was just a natural progression of my continued healing and self-care. But

when she started to belittle, shame, or humiliate me, I ended our phone calls firmly and quickly.

When we get to acceptance, we can determine which of our mother's behaviors we're willing to put up with, how we'll deal with them, and for how long. Isn't that amazing?

Takeaways

- Narcissistic Grief Awareness happens when we become aware of our mother's narcissism and begin to realize how it impacted us.

- There are six phases to work through in narcissistic grief awareness.

- The phases are not experienced in any particular order, and it's possible to become stuck in one and not progress forward without some assistance.

- We can't get to the final phase of acceptance without working through the previous five stages.

Action for Healing

Make a section in your journal, just for writing about your feelings of grief. Write at length about the feelings you're experiencing as you enter the phases of narcissistic awareness grief. Include these topics:

1. Denial: How does it feel when you think of your mother as a narcissist? Do you feel bad about yourself? In what way? Is it important for you to protect your mother's image? Is it more important to protect your mother than to face some uncomfortable truths about her and also about yourself? Explain.

2. Feelings of betrayal

3. Confusion

4. Rejection

5. Shame: Write about what you're ashamed of.

6. Anger: At whom? Why?

7. Fear: What are you afraid of? Give a best- and worst-case scenario for each thing that you fear. Does the fear decrease when you do this? Why do you think that is?

8. Abandonment

9. Loneliness and isolation: Talk about how these feel. Can you think of ways to feel reconnected?

PART II
GOT LEMONS?

Chapter Eight
THE NARCISSISTIC MOTHER

"The eyes see only what the mind is prepared to comprehend."

–Henri Bergson

So far, we've taken a look at narcissism and its definition according to the DSM-5, the diagnostic criteria, and it's types and subtypes. We've seen its characteristics and how they present themselves and learned something about how trauma, including that of narcissistic abuse, impacts the human brain.

TRAITS OF A NARCISSISTIC MOTHER

I think the hardest thing to understand, for those who haven't experienced maternal narcissism, is that narcissistic parents don't see their children as individuals. A narcissistic mother doesn't see her children as independently functioning human beings who have their own thoughts and feelings. She doesn't see their individual personalities or acknowledge their goals.

A narcissistic mother sees her kids as extensions of herself. Because of that, to her, everything the kids do and say reflects on *her*. She makes everything about *her*. The kids are simply satellites who learn at a very young age that they're expected to contribute positively to their mother's image. They understand that every decision and every action they take must happen within those parameters, or there will be ugly consequences.

When a narcissistic mother doesn't like aspects of her personality, she emotionally separates herself from those qualities and then projects those unacceptable traits onto one of her children. She will then mistreat that child for "having" those qualities. When she does this, she's using a defense mechanism known as projection, which is what occurs when we attribute a trait that we dislike in ourselves as being another person's, not our own (Brenner 2019). The mother now has reason to blame the child for anything she thinks, does, or says that she finds objectionable within herself, but is unwilling to admit or change.

"Even perceived rejection activates the brain's pain centers."

Introducing: Scapegoating

When a narcissistic mom uses projection to protect her ego from her unlikeable qualities, there is a risk of neglect, maltreatment, abuse, blame, shame, or even physical violence to the children as a result. She'll play a game of "whose fault is it? I know it's not mine" (Brenner et al. 2018). Because narcissistic mothers are so controlling, they need to have reasons that explain undesirable happenings, and they insist on having a person to hold accountable. This phenomenon is known as scapegoating. The scapegoating practice happens in dysfunctional families, with the role of the scapegoat being either temporary or permanent. The scapegoat is the fall guy, the person who gets blamed for offenses and injustices that happen to anyone in the family. Family members, except for the narcissistic mom, often take turns playing the scapegoat role, and at any given time, the mom determines who the scapegoat is.

Tactics like scapegoating are all attempts of the mother to maintain control. When a narcissistic mom feels like she's losing control over her kids, she will often lash out in vengeful ways, subtly or with direct hostility. Narcissistic mothers are highly reactive to any threat or challenge to their power. They have a sense of entitlement, ownership, and possession of their kids.

MANIPULATIVE TACTICS

There is a multitude of ways that a narcissistic mother can emotionally injure her children. I believe these behaviors are the result of other, often unrelated issues, such as:

1. She's not articulate or doesn't have a strong vocabulary, so she's not able to accurately express or describe what she's thinking or feeling.

2. She doesn't know how to identify her emotions.

3. She hasn't had an emotionally healthy upbringing, or she hasn't witnessed emotionally healthy relationships.

4. She's emotionally immature and can't regulate her emotions.

5. She hasn't personally experienced or learned strong parenting skills.

Narcissistic mothers manipulate and control their children in a variety of ways:

- Withholding affection, affirmation, validation, attention, encouragement, praise, and other self-esteem building behaviors

- Exhibiting intense and scary displays of emotion and drama ("narcissistic rages")

- Verbally abusing them with insults, criticism, and name-calling

- Threatening violence (may or may not be carried out)

- Maintaining a victim mentality

- Rejection

- Lying

- Giving the "silent treatment" as a form of punishment

- Exercising a "selective memory"

- Gaslighting to control perceptions and memories

I'm personally familiar with all of these tactics. Gaslighting is the one that harmed me the most. It's an extremely emotionally and mentally destructive form of manipulation.

Even though most of the above-listed behaviors are not physically hurtful, each one can activate the pain centers in the human brain. Research in the field of neuroscience shows us that even perceived rejection activates the area of the brain where pain is felt (Eisenberger et al. 2004). The point is that verbal abuse, threats, rejection, and other forms of emotional mistreatment do *hurt* us.

Takeaways

- A narcissistic mother sees her kids as extensions of herself, and everything they do reflects on *her*.

- When a narcissistic mother doesn't like aspects of her personality, she emotionally separates herself from those qualities and then "projects" those unacceptable traits onto one or more of her children.

- A narcissistic mother can emotionally hurt or injure her children in a variety of ways.

Action for Healing

1. Have you been a target of projection? In what way has your mother used projection to see her own unacceptable traits within you?

2. Do you think your mother has intentionally hurt you? Explain.

3. The first step in healing is acknowledging that you grew up in a dysfunctional family. You may be reluctant to do this because it may feel painful or shameful. It may stir up painful memories that you'd rather keep buried. If these statements are true for you, I encourage you to go at your own pace, continue writing in your journal, and give yourself time and space for self-reflection and beginning the grieving process.

4. You may be feeling denial, fear, confusion, shame, rejection, loneliness, abandonment, or any number and combination of

emotions. These feelings are all an expected part of acknowledging what's happened. The grieving process begins with feelings.

Chapter Nine
THE NARCISSISTIC ABUSE CYCLE

"Adult children frequently describe their narcissistic mother as being self-centered, judgmental, fake, dishonest, childish, manipulative, and mean."

—Karyl McBride, 2013

When I was a domestic violence counselor, we used the term "cycle of abuse" to describe the patterns of behavior that led up to and included an abusive event. As counselors, we taught women who were involved in abusive relationships to recognize these patterns and to identify which stage they were currently in. By doing this, they could create a preemptive strategy to avoid or cope with an upcoming abusive incident.

Dr. Lenore Walker proposed the cycle of abuse in 1979. After interviewing 1,500 female domestic violence survivors, she found that they all shared a similar abusive scenario and that there was a recognizable pattern to how the abusive events happened. Dr. Walker developed the "cycle of abuse" based on this scenario.

FOUR ELEMENTS OF ABUSE

Four elements were present in various forms for each of the female abuse survivors:

1. Tension Building

2. Abusive Incident

3. Remorse

4. Honeymoon

The Honeymoon Period proceeds directly into Tension Building, and the cycle repeats itself, uninterrupted. Every cycle shares the same four phases, but each cycle's details differ from the previous ones. From one abuse cycle to the next, each of the four stages, as well as the cycle itself, can last different amounts of time or include behaviors that are unique from those of the last time.

The following diagram is based on Walker's Cycle of Abuse.

1. Tension Building   # 2. Abusive Incident

4. Honeymoon   # 3. Remorse

(Walker, L.E.,1979)

The first phase is the "Tension Building" period. In it, the target senses growing strain in the relationship, and becomes anxious, highly alert, and guarded. There is an unshakeable feeling that there will be an abusive incident soon. Hence, the target attempts to control the environment to keep the abuser happy and calm.

In phase two, the abusive incident occurs. The abuse may be physical, mental, spiritual, emotional, verbal, or financial. Examples include name-calling, gaslighting, threats, intimidation, angry outbursts, arguing, blaming, and withholding love, affection, and attention.

The third phase is the "Remorse" period. In this phase, the abuser apologizes, makes excuses, and promises that the abuse will never happen again. The target is showered with love, affection, and attention, and sometimes offered gifts and tokens of affection as indicators of sorrow.

The "Honeymoon" is the fourth phase. There is a period of calm in the relationship while the abuser attempts to make the target feel loved, safe, and secure. The Honeymoon will continue for an undetermined amount of time, the length of which may change with every cycle.

This entire cycle will continuously repeat, often over years, until it is intentionally interrupted by one of the two participants. One way of interrupting the cycle is for the target to leave the relationship.

When a narcissist is involved in the cycle of abuse, it plays out differently. The "Remorse" phase is *not present* in the narcissistic abuse cycle because narcissists are unwilling to accept responsibility and would instead place the blame on their target.

Remember, narcissists need to feel superior and "right" in every situation. This, combined with their lack of empathy, means that they don't experience feelings of remorse. Remorsefulness requires empathy, sympathy, and taking responsibility for our actions (Hammond 2018).

So, the narcissistic cycle of abuse differs significantly from Walker's cycle of abuse in this phase.

THE NARCISSISTIC CYCLE OF ABUSE

Here is what the cycle of abuse looks like when a narcissist is the offender. This diagram is based on Christine Hammond's "Narcissistic Cycle of Abuse."

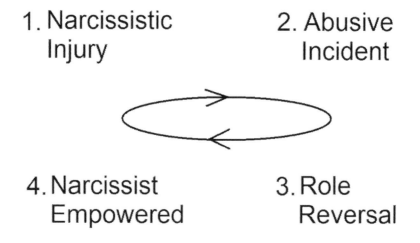

1. Narcissistic Injury   2. Abusive Incident

4. Narcissist Empowered   3. Role Reversal

(Hammond, C. 2018)

In phase one, a Narcissistic Injury occurs. The abuser feels rejected, threatened, jealous, abandoned, disrespected, or any feeling that challenges their superiority. The target feels anxious and tries to appease and please the narcissist, much like in phase one of Walker's Cycle of Abuse.

As in Walker's Cycle of Abuse, phase two is also an Abusive Incident, which could be physical, mental, spiritual, emotional, verbal, or financial. Examples include name-calling, gaslighting, threats, intimidation, angry outbursts, arguing, blaming, withholding love, affection, and attention.

Phase three is completely different in the Narcissistic Cycle of Abuse. When the cycle involves a narcissist, the roles in the Remorse stage are reversed. Now the narcissistic mom will play the part of the abused/victim, and the target will apologize and appease. What eventually happens in the fourth phase is that narcissistic behaviors become stronger, and the abuse cycle repeats until someone intentionally breaks the cycle. To break it, the target needs to change their behavior by not accepting the role reversal. In other words, the target will no longer take the blame or accept the role of the abuser.

SUBTLETIES OF ABUSE: GOLDEN, INVISIBLE AND SCAPEGOAT

As I mentioned earlier, there's a particularly dysfunctional family dynamic in which one of the narcissist's children becomes "idealized" and is the clear parental favorite, known as the "Golden Child." Any other children will take turns being devalued and blamed. They're known as the "Invisible Child" and the "Scapegoat" (Streep 2017). The narcissist-mom controls these roles.

The roles of the Golden Child, Invisible Child, and Scapegoat are flexible. Any part can be assigned to any child at any time, depending on the narcissist's mood. It's a "crazy-making" situation because the narcissist-mom has the unchallenged power to change the entire family dynamic quickly and unpredictably. For those of us in this position, it catches us unaware and unprepared.

The Golden Child: The Golden Child's role is to bring positive attention to the mother and the family. The Golden Child is the favorite, and as such, may have a special status and receive more attention and praise. They're the ones that get bragged about. They make the narcissistic mom look great as a mother. Even so, she will always take some credit for their accomplishments. When they walk into the room, mom's focus is on them. Golden Children may grow up to be adults who are compulsive overachievers or perfectionists who feel a loss of identity and have low self-esteem.

"Forms of idealizing include praise, attention, and bragging. Types of devaluing include criticizing, blaming, shaming, lying about, lying to, intentionally frightening, projecting, and gaslighting."

The Invisible Child (aka Lost Child): The role of the Invisible Child is to "stay under the radar," to follow the rules unquestioningly, be quiet, and easy-going. Invisible Children are often taken for granted, and their needs are neglected because they never complain or ask for anything. Invisible Children may internalize a sense of having no impact on others, or their input not mattering. They may grow up to feel insignificant and inconsequential because their sense of identity has not fully developed (Stines, 2018).

The Scapegoat: The Scapegoat's role is to bear the blame for all of the family's problems. They are the butt of jokes and get less of everything than the other siblings. They are seen as the problem child. Scapegoats often grow up to become the ones who speak up and challenge the dysfunction. They're the ones telling the truth about what's going on in the family and will act out the frustration, anger, and feelings of the entire family (Cole 2019).

When we suddenly and unexpectedly become the Scapegoat, it leaves us wondering what the heck just happened. Was it something I said (or didn't mention or was supposed to mention)? Was it something I did (or didn't do or did but not correctly)? If not me, then who or what was it? Was it another family member? A friend? Her boss? The traffic? Did something happen at work? Was it the weather? Maybe it was a coworker. Or her supervisor. Perhaps it was the cat? Or something she got (or didn't get) in the mail?

When I found myself in the Scapegoat position, I could literally spend hours trying to figure out why. I wanted and needed to fix it, or at least to understand what had so hugely affected my position within the family. I wanted to attempt to control it and not let it happen again.

A sudden change in family positions is upsetting. These random role reversals affect our sense of observation, decision-making, and self-trust because we never know if the explanation we're giving ourselves is accurate. And we're continuously guessing our current standing within the family. And if we're the Golden Child, we're also appeasing and pleasing our mom because we don't want to lose that privilege.

"Narcissistic mothers revel in generating competition between their children and emotionally distancing them from one another."

Living with a narcissistic mother has been described as "living in a war zone." Those of us who've lived under those circumstances were usually on high alert, in fight-or-flight survival mode, because we had no idea when the next attack or role reversal would happen. It meant we were continuously producing stress hormones like adrenaline and cortisol, so it was a common occurrence to feel confused or experience scattered thinking, have difficulty making decisions, or remember. Eventually, we became emotionally and physically exhausted.

There are other subtle ways that narcissistic mothers attempt to control or manipulate their children:

- Belittling, criticizing, and name-calling

- Patronizing and being condescending

- Publicly or privately embarrassing their children

- Threatening their children in some way

- Ordering their children to do things, taking away their choices

- Controlling money or access to it

- Monitoring and controlling whereabouts

- Exhibiting scary, emotional outbursts

- Acting on jealousy

- Using manipulative or guilt-inducing ploys

- Isolating children from friends, family members, or social connections

- Being indifferent to her children's needs

- Denying or trivializing feelings

Any combination of these behaviors can result in lowering or destroying a child's self-esteem and cause them to feel unnecessary fear and shame (McBride 2018).

STIRRING THE POT

A narcissistic mother revels in generating competition between her children and emotionally distancing them from one another. These moms enjoy creating distrust, doubt, insecurity, competition, and resentment between siblings. As I've mentioned, this is called triangulation. It's a manipulative tactic used to control information or interactions between individuals.

A therapist once suggested that triangulation was a form of entertainment for my mom. She liked creating drama. She'd stir up trouble, then sit back and enjoy the show. For example, my mom would say one thing to me, putting a specific person in a negative light, and then she'd provide a slightly different version, with me as the "bad guy," to the other person. When we sensed that something negative was happening between us, but not of our own doing, the other person and I began communicating directly with each other. We compared the different versions of my mother's stories and soon came to realize that we were being manipulated seemingly for my mother's amusement. I informed my mother that we were aware of what she was doing. Of course, she flipped the scenario, instantly becoming the innocent victim, but the triangulation stopped pretty much immediately.

Takeaways

- The abuse cycle defined by Dr. Walker has four stages: Tension Building, Abusive Incident, Remorsefulness, and the Honeymoon Phase. The cycle will continuously repeat until either the abuser or the target changes their way of interacting.

- In the narcissistic abuse cycle, the roles in the "Remorsefulness" stage get reversed. A narcissist- mom will play the part of the victim, and the mistreated child/children will appease and apologize.

- In dysfunctional families, there's a dynamic where family members are assigned roles of the Golden Child, Invisible Child, and Scapegoat. Any part can be attributed to any child at any time by the mother.

- A narcissistic mother revels in generating competition between her children and emotionally distancing them from one another.

Action for Healing

1. Have you witnessed the narcissistic abuse cycle in your own family? If so, in which stage is the family currently? Create a section in your journal for monitoring the cycle. What have you noticed? Using what you've learned so far, what do you think will happen next?

2. Do you see the Golden, Invisible, and Scapegoat roles played in your family? What role are you currently in? What other roles have you played? Give examples.

3. How can you stop feeling like a victim in these family dynamics? Look for a counselor or support group, where you can safely share your thoughts and emotions and learn how to set boundaries.

Chapter Ten
NARCISSISTIC LYING

"False face must hide what the false heart doth know."

—William Shakespeare, *Macbeth*

All human beings lie. Our reasons and motives for lying and the types of lies we tell are all as different as the people who tell them, but there are two kinds of lies.

KINDHEARTED LIES

We tell kindhearted (aka face-saving or prosocial) lies to prevent someone's feelings from being hurt, to save a relationship, or keep ourselves from losing status. We do it because we feel empathy, and because in certain circumstances, lying may make us appear to be kind or caring.

Have you ever done this? For example, your friend says she's been told she wears too much makeup. You know that this statement felt unkind and hurtful to her, so even though you agree that she wears too much makeup, you smile and tell her she absolutely does not! You lie because you don't want to hurt her feelings, knowing that she's already hurt from the previous remark. You also want to avoid her becoming angry at you because that would cause problems in your friendship.

Self-serving Lies

We tell self-serving (aka egocentric lies) to enhance our feeling of well-being, to achieve a goal, or to avoid potential humiliation. Have you ever told a self-serving lie? For example, you were supposed to make a veggie dip to take to your office meeting. Since you didn't have time to make it the night before, you wake early and go to the grocery store so you can pick up a homemade-looking dip from the deli. You put it in a bowl and pass it off as your own, to save face (Neal 2017).

Narcissistic lying is different, and narcissists lie *a lot*. The fundamental difference is their motivation for lying. The current theory is that all narcissistic behaviors, including lying, are unconsciously motivated by shame and driven by previous narcissistic injuries. Lying is central to a narcissist's identity, but because all of their experiences are filtered through previous injuries, they'll view the lie as being the truth. In his book "The Narcissist You Know," Dr. Joseph Burgo says about the narcissist, "He doesn't see himself as a liar but rather as an embattled defender of the 'truth' as he has come to see it" (Burgo 2016).

> *"Narcissistic behaviors, including lying, are unconsciously motivated by shame and driven by previous narcissistic injuries."*

Narcissistic Lies

A narcissistic mother's lies are a combination of her character traits and her life experiences, so there's usually a small "kernel" of truth in each lie. It'll be difficult and confusing to try to find that kernel, but your intuition will tell you it's there. In her story, in addition to lying, she'll also exaggerate any information that makes her look "good," and she'll just as easily minimize information that has the potential to make her look "bad."

Because narcissists need to believe that they're always correct and never make mistakes, they often have difficulty knowing the difference between lies and the truth. It makes absolute sense if you remember that a narcissist's entire life is a lie because of their false face. They have grandiose beliefs about their false selves, and they need validation and affirmation for those beliefs. The false self keeps the narcissist feeling superior, and that's essential for them to avoid narcissistic injuries. They see anything that threatens their superiority as an attack and will respond per se.

Narcissists need to lie and to have the lies believed, or there will be hell to pay, often in the form of a narcissistic rage or the silent treatment.

Takeaways

- All human beings lie. Our reasons and motives for lying and the types of lies we tell are all as different as the people who tell them.

- A narcissistic mother's lies are a combination of her character and life experiences, so there's usually a small kernel of truth in each lie.

- Narcissists need to believe they're always correct, that they never make mistakes, so they often have a hard time telling the difference between their own lies and the truth.

- Narcissistic behaviors, including lying, are unconsciously motivated by shame and driven by previous narcissistic injuries.

Action for Healing

The more you learn about the impact of maternal narcissism on your life, the more you may want to deny that you were a target of such behavior. Use your journal to continue writing about your feelings and discoveries. Look at your childhood family dynamics, as well as your relationship with your mom.

Answer these questions:

1. Have you ever lied? What kind of lie was it? What was your motivation? Whom or what (for example, a relationship) did the lie hurt?

2. Has your mother ever lied to you? What kind of lie was it? What do you think her motivation was? Whom or what did it hurt?

    a. Did you believe the lie? Why or why not?

    b. Do you still believe the lie? Why or why not? What can you choose to believe instead?

Chapter Eleven
THE SILENT TREATMENT

"Remove the veils so I might see what is really happening here and not be intoxicated by my stories and my fears."

—Elizabeth Lesser

Narcissistic moms love the silent treatment. It's their secret weapon when they want to manipulate and hurt in a big way. Using the silent treatment is a way to inflict pain without causing visible evidence.

Research shows that when we ignore or exclude someone, it activates the same part of their brain as physical pain does. Narcissists instinctively know that this manipulative technique is extremely hurtful. It's traumatic to those it's inflicted upon (Eisenberger et al. 2004).

As I've noted, a narcissistic mother gets her sense of self through her children, and she needs to protect her self-image and her reputation as a loving, caring mother. Her children are a necessary part of her identity. This is why the silent treatment is so meaningful to her. To a narcissistic mother, when she uses the silent treatment, it's as if she's cutting off a very displeasing part of herself and, at the same time, understands how painful it feels to the person she's shunning. I've heard others remark that my mother was the kind of person who would cut off her nose to spite her face. Win at any cost, right?

THE STONE WALL

The silent treatment is a punishment that consists of "hurt and rescue." It can continue for months or even years and is often used to teach a lesson or to manipulate behavior (Eisenberger et al. 2004). For those of us who've been subjected to this form of abuse, it kept us anxious by triggering our fear of abandonment. (Saeed, K. 2019).

When I was seventeen, I endured my mother's silent treatment for a little over three months. She had given me the silent treatment before, and she would again, but this instance lasted the longest. For the entire three months, I was met with stony silence any time I attempted to interact with her. She would not make eye contact with me. There was no acknowledgment that I existed whatsoever.

I broke our silent relationship now and again, testing to see if she would respond, and each time I was met with cold rejection. The message was loud and clear that she was not finished punishing me, and my attempts were not going to have an effect. It was as if I was invisible. I remember needing affirmation that others could see me and that I existed. I felt like I was heading into insanity.

One day, as mysteriously as the silent treatment had started, it ended. When my mother broke the silence and spoke to me, it was some little unimportant phrase that had no real significance, but it indicated the shunning was over.

I couldn't figure out what I had done to offend or anger my mother, to cause her to take such extreme action as the silent treatment. I spent an excessive amount of time obsessing about it, replaying scenarios and conversations repeatedly, looking for the cause. I never found it, and of course, we never discussed what happened. If I was supposed to learn a lesson, I never knew what it was. Maybe the whole thing was nothing more than a show of power, meant to demoralize and unsettle me. It remains a mystery to this day.

PUNITIVE SILENCE

When a person is actively ignored, it causes such psychological and emotional anguish that it can actually be seen on brain scans (Pune Mirror 2019). The silent treatment triggers a fear of abandonment, which is very frightening, but for children like me who'd already been abandoned by one parent, it is unbearable. I was obsessed with thoughts like, "Who will take care of me?" "Will I ever matter?" "Will I ever be safe?" "Will anyone ever love me?"

The fear of abandonment causes anxiety, worry, sleep loss, and inability to concentrate. Imagine trying to learn in school or study for tests while being actively ignored and rejected by a parent. With every silent treatment, we go deeper into survival mode, and we can experience panic attacks, appetite loss, binge-eating, racing heartbeat, nightmares, depression, confusion, and obsessive thinking. With each, we learn to focus more on our mother's behavior and her needs. We learn to provide what she needs and wants because we fear we'll be emotionally or physically abandoned again. The need to please and appease her becomes overblown.

"The silent treatment is a punishment that consists of a "hurt and rescue" cycle."

A narcissistic mom understands that she'll get away with rejecting and shunning because, as children, we have no choice but to welcome her back when she decides to return to our lives. We need her, after all, and she knows it. When she's ready to acknowledge us again, we're so happy, aren't we?

The narcissistic mom likes knowing how hurt we are by her silent treatment. Our pain demonstrates to her that she is all-powerful and can devastate us if and when she chooses. It's a great form of narcissistic supply.

Every time we go through the silent treatment, we're diminished. Each time we endure active ignoring, we question our self-worth. Our self-esteem and self-image are further eroded, and our fear of abandonment escalates. Despite our accomplishments, acknowledgments, or friendships, we find ourselves desperate for our mother's approval, which is, of course, *always* out of reach. We may come close, but we never quite make it.

We eventually accept that we aren't worthy of her love or attention. We settle for any crumbs of affection or attention we can get from her. We learn that we're somehow inferior and will never be able to please her, although we should continue trying.

This repeated process is called "trauma bonding" and is another example of the powerful emotional bonds created between abuser and abused. Over time, trauma bonds become very resistant to change, and a codependent relationship develops.

TAKEAWAYS

- Narcissistic moms love the silent treatment, and it's their secret weapon when they want to manipulate and hurt.

- A narcissistic mother gets her sense of self through her children. Her children are a necessary part of her identity.

- The silent treatment is a "hurt and rescue" type of cycle. It's meant to keep us anxious by triggering our fear of abandonment.

- When we're actively ignored, it causes such psychological and emotional anguish that it can be seen on brain scans.

- Trauma bonding occurs when two people become deeply connected by going through cycles of abuse together.

ACTION FOR HEALING

1. Have you experienced the silent treatment? By whom? Create a section in your journal to write specifically about this event:

    a. Who stopped speaking to you? Why? How did you feel about it? How long did it last? How was the silent treatment ended?

2. Have trusting, open conversations with your therapist or support group about your childhood memories. Determine to let go of the dysfunctional family rules of "Don't Talk, Don't

Trust, Don't Feel." Silence keeps the issues hidden and doesn't benefit anybody.

Chapter Twelve
SHAME

"Shame is the intensely painful feeling or experience of believing we are flawed and therefore unworthy of acceptance and belonging."

—Brené Brown

The shame of enduring mistreatment or abuse from our mothers leaves long-lasting scars.

IT'S ABOUT CONTROL

Shaming is a method of control that's interwoven throughout the abuse cycle. Shaming can be accomplished with mixed messages, sarcasm, scapegoating, narcissistic rages, gaslighting, and trauma bonding, to name a few. *One thing is for sure: you'll find active shaming wherever there is a narcissist.*

Shame tells you that everyone is judging you as unforgivingly as you judge yourself. Shame lies. It says that you're unworthy of acceptance or belonging; that you deserve insults, criticisms, rejection, and loneliness. Shame says that you're not good enough.

The word "abuse" is full of shame. Using that word regarding childhood experiences feels like a massive exaggeration of what happened and a handy but sad excuse for unresolved issues. When we use the word "abuse," it feels like attention and sympathy-seeking. It feels like "poor me; I'm a helpless victim."

We may intentionally minimize our painful childhood experiences because we don't want to think of our mothers as "abusers" or ourselves as unwitting targets. Having those kinds of thoughts can cause us to feel more ashamed, and that affects our core identity. Those of us who've experienced traumatic childhood events due to our mother's narcissism may feel a sense of disgust or humiliation in addition to shame, and we see ourselves in a negative light when we compare ourselves with others.

In her book, "I Thought It Was Just Me (But It Isn't): Making the Journey from 'What Will People Think?' to 'I Am Enough,'" Brené Brown discusses shame as a "silent epidemic" and something that everybody experiences at some point (2008).

Why does a narcissistic mom shame her children? Remember that narcissists need to feel superior, and shaming her children allows a narcissistic mother to put herself in an untouchable status. Shaming also minimizes possible future threats, like expressing embarrassing comments or thoughts about her.

A narcissistic mother will shame her children for other reasons as well. All of them have to do with making her feel invincible while decreasing her children's self-confidence, self-esteem, and enjoyment of life.

METHODS OF SHAMING

A narcissistic mother can shame her children in a variety of ways:

1. *Changing the narrative:* After a child attains an accomplishment, the narcissistic mom will tell the story of the achievement, and she'll add a shameful twist to it. If asked, she'll jokingly say she did it because she doesn't want her child to become self-important or to have a "big head," but really, it is intended to humiliate.

2. *Breaking confidences:* Narcissists love to gain embarrassing or humiliating information about their children to use later, so they appear important or more intelligent. A narcissistic mom will keep her child anxious about the possibility that she may share this upsetting information with others.

3. *Pointing out flaws:* Narcissists believe they have no faults but are very good at identifying those of others. They enjoy shaming their children by passive-aggressively devaluing them. A narcissistic mom might say, "I was only joking" or "You're too sensitive" if her child is hurt by this behavior.

4. *Playing the victim:* As we've seen, narcissists love to be the victim in their version of reality. A narcissistic mom will purposefully frustrate her child and then use their exasperation to justify flipping the scenario and becoming the victim herself. Then she'll openly deem her child's frustrated response as a shameful thing.

5. *Blaming:* Narcissists don't take responsibility for their actions. When a narcissistic mom makes a mistake or if something unexpected goes wrong, she'll place blame on her child. The child has no power to prevent this and can't change it. It is a no-win situation.

6. *Belittling:* Narcissists are typically condescending and belittle their children by talking down to them, calling them names,

implying that they're jealous or insecure, or telling their adult children to "grow up." Narcissistic moms enjoy giving the impression that they've developed beyond the level that others have.

7. *Laying on religious guilt:* Every religion has standards and expectations, and a narcissistic mom will use them to guilt her children into behaving in a particular manner. She may say she's praying about the child's behavior, or that she's asking for God's intercession because the child's behavior is that displeasing to her.

8. *Using aggressive tactics:* Narcissists personally attack others to make them defensive. Defensive people become highly alert to protect themselves. A narcissistic mom will use defensiveness as a sign of guilt. She'll accuse her children of wrongdoing even when there hasn't been any.

9. *Playing the expert:* Narcissists will sometimes speak authoritatively above a person's level of understanding or knowledge. They do this to make the person feel inferior. A narcissistic mother will do this to be seen as an authority figure. She'll use her vocabulary, posture (looking down), and the elaboration of details as a way of shaming. The message is that she is smarter and more knowledgeable than you'll ever be.

10. Comparing: As a result of their need to feel superior, narcissists act as though they've already outperformed everyone else. They insist they said or did "it" first, and much better. By outdoing her children, a narcissistic mom minimizes their accomplishments, which supports their belief of not being good enough.

11. *Physical appearance:* Narcissists like to appear physically intimidating or untouchable. They love attention and admiration, so they often dress to get noticed. They may even use their physical appearance as a way to demean and shame others. For example, an athletic narcissistic mom will make hurtful comments to her children about their bodies as compared to her own.

12. *Expectations (using "should" or "ought"):* A narcissistic mom will frequently play the game of, "I told you so" by reminding her children that they didn't heed her advice. For example, "You should've taken your boots as I told you to. Now your shoes are ruined."

13. *Manipulation:* Narcissists don't ask directly for what they want because it feels like weakness. They don't want to feel indebted to anyone. They gain an intense feeling of power by controlling and influencing others. They prefer that to openness.

14. *Gaslighting:* Narcissists like to control other's beliefs, feelings, thoughts, and perceptions. To do this, they "rewrite" past events casting themselves as either the good guy or the victim. If others disagree with the revised version, the narcissist will mock, humiliate, dismiss their memory as faulty, or say something equally shaming.

15. *Dog whistling:* This tactic is a form of gaslighting and manipulating. It gets its name from the device called a dog-whistle that, because of it's pitch, can only be heard by dogs. When using the dog-whistle approach, a narcissistic mother will use coded language. Her words will mean one thing to her audience, but something entirely different and hurtful for her child. For example, mom knows that her overweight adult child is

embarrassed by her size. When they're together, the mom will gush about how great her child's *friend* looks after losing weight.

16. *Sandbagging:* Purposely appearing weak or less informed to deceive someone is called sandbagging. Narcissists often manipulate others by faking weaknesses. A narcissistic mom may pretend to be ill to shame her child. For example, she wants her adult child to visit. Instead of simply inviting them over, she pretends to be sick, so the adult child feels pressured into making an appearance.

"Shame is the most powerful, master emotion. It's the fear that we're not good enough."

—Brené Brown

ABOUT FORGIVENESS

Have you considered forgiving your mother? Or is that idea outrageous? Maybe your wounds are still fresh, or it feels too soon, or impossible. It would be a good idea to consider it at some point.

You see, forgiveness doesn't mean that your mom will get away with her hurtful behavior or have no repercussions. Forgiveness is a decision you make when you're ready to release the resentment and anger you feel. It's extended whether she asks for it or not, or whether she "deserves" to be forgiven. Forgiving doesn't mean forgetting what she did or condoning her behavior. Forgiveness is for you, not your mother.

Offering forgiveness affords peace and freedom from destructive anger. It means empowering yourself by letting go of your negative feelings toward her. By forgiving, you can acknowledge your pain without letting it define you so you can truly heal and move forward. Your mother will face the naturally occurring consequences for her actions, but those aren't for you to determine or carry out. You're learning to let go of controlling outcomes and consequences and other codependent behaviors like that.

"Vulnerability is not winning or losing; it's having the courage to show up and be seen when we have no control over the outcome."

—Brené Brown

If you're too angry to forgive right now, continue to acknowledge and validate your angry feelings and resentments. Doing this can help you see where your boundaries need to be.

TAKEAWAYS

- A narcissist mother shames her children in a multitude of ways.

- You may intentionally minimize your painful childhood experiences because you don't want to think of your mothers as an "abuser" or yourself as a target of abuse.

- Shaming her children allows a narcissistic mother to feel superior and minimizes future threats, like embarrassing comments they may make about her.

ACTION FOR HEALING

1. Have you experienced feelings of shame? When did it start? Are you still ashamed? What are you ashamed of?

2. Explain what, how, and why you felt or still feel ashamed. In looking at these incidents with a fresh perspective, how do you think about and understand them now?

3. Do you feel ready to forgive? Even if you're not, I suggest being open to the possibility. Read about forgiveness and learn how it would benefit you. Remember, the benefits of forgiveness are for you, not your mother.

4. If you haven't reached out to a counselor or support group, now would be a great time to pursue that. Some counselors offer a sliding-fee scale, meaning that you pay what you can afford according to your income.

5. I highly suggest Brené Brown's books on vulnerability and shame: "I Thought It Was Just Me (But It Isn't)—Making the Journey from 'What Will People Think' to 'I Am Enough'" and "The Power of Vulnerability: Teachings of Authenticity, Connection, and Courage."

* * *

MS. BROWN ALSO HAS TWO EXCELLENT TED TALKS ON THE TOPICS OF VULNERABILITY AND SHAME:

—The Power of Vulnerability:
ted.com/talks/brene_brown_the_power_of_vulnerability
—Listening to Shame:
ted.com/talks/brene_brown_listening_to_shame

Chapter Thirteen
NARCISSISTIC SUPPLY

"What you allow is what will continue."

−Unknown

EMOTIONAL FOOD

The concept of "narcissistic supply" was first introduced to the field of psychoanalytic theory by Otto Fenichel in 1938. The term defines the admiration narcissists need to keep their self-esteem intact. They need to take this supply of approval from the people in their environment, so their false face can survive.

Remember, narcissists don't view people as unique individuals with their own needs, feelings, goals, or lives. To narcissists, people are simply props who play a supporting role in their lives. A narcissist's only concern is what they can get from others or what others can do for them. They have difficulty emotionally bonding with others because relationships are all about power, control, and the benefits they can obtain.

Like any narcissist, a narcissistic mom cannot survive without supply. It's her emotional food; any form of attention, affirmation, approval, or admiration she gets from her kids will suffice. She feels a sense of power and importance from any emotional reaction, any emotion—fear, sadness, anger, shame, whatever—will do because it feeds her false self, making it stronger.

WHY DO THEY NEED IT?

Securing a supply keeps her false face working in an automatic cycle: project the false self, receive the supply, empower and strengthen the false self, repeat.

The cycle repeats itself because it provides feelings of power, control, and importance. Narcissists thrive on these, feeling formidable, even omnipotent after getting supply. This leads to a narcissistic high, which potentially makes her dangerous. You won't be permitted to share your thoughts or feelings when your narcissist-mom is on a high. She won't take any challenge lightly and will go for the jugular to prove her supremacy. She's not interested in what you have to say or how you feel. It's all about her.

"Acquaintances, friends, and extended family of a narcissist-mom often don't see the narcissism for what it is. They believe she is a kind and loving person because that's what she displays."

After going through this cycle a few times, we get it. We understand that she's more powerful than we are—that it's always about "winning," and she'll be delighted to win at our expense. In her mind, she's always right, and there's no use trying to have a conversation or share an opinion because she'll become combative. Eventually, we'll likely end up feeling defeated, unloved, and insignificant. We'll learn to walk on eggshells and to placate, please, and pacify her. We'll anticipate her needs and moods and act accordingly. Do you remember what that's called? That's right. Codependency.

WHY WE SEE WHAT'S HAPPENING, AND OTHERS DON'T

Acquaintances, friends, and extended family of a narcissist-mom often don't see the narcissism for what it is. They believe she is a kind and loving person because that's what she displays for them. At home, it's a different story. We, as her closest family, get to experience what she is really like, firsthand. We can see both of her faces—the false and the real.

Adult children of narcissists (ACNs) often express a shared and frustrating quandary: How do we get people to understand or even believe what's going on when our mother's public "false face" is so very different from what we're familiar with at home?

A narcissistic mom usually reveals her true self during a time of crisis, conflict, or high stress. When she's pressured, and it's hard for her to control her emotions, her lack of empathy is exposed. When she feels threatened, she'll go for the "win," by protecting herself. What's said or done won't matter. Winning matters. High-pressure situations show how shallow her emotional connections are. Our shame, humiliation, and embarrassment are her narcissistic supply.

Takeaways

- The admiration a narcissist needs to feel to keep their self-esteem intact is called narcissistic supply. They take this admiration and support from the people in their environment.

- A narcissistic mom cannot survive without narcissistic supply, which is like emotional food. Any emotional reaction, positive or negative, we give a narcissistic mother can be a form of supply.

- Acquaintances, friends, and extended family often don't see the narcissism for what it is.

- A narcissistic mom usually reveals her true self during a time of crisis, conflict, or high stress.

Action for Healing

1. Have you been a source of narcissistic supply? How? Write about it.

2. Will that change now that you are aware of the dynamic? How?

3. What, if anything, has contributed to your becoming a source of supply?

Chapter Fourteen
TRAUMA BONDING

"Betrayal is a more subtle, twisted feeling than terror. It burns and eats, but terror stabs right through."

—Wendy Hoffman

THE TIES THAT BIND

If you've ever known someone who's consistently mistreated but won't physically leave the relationship, you may find some understanding here about why that is.

Trauma Bonding is an intense emotional connection between an abusive person (abuser) and their target (victim). "Trauma bonds are dysfunctional attachments that occur in the presence of danger, shame, or exploitation" (Carnes 2016).

Trauma bonding is also a survival mechanism.

In a trauma bond, the target becomes emotionally attached to the abuser, feeling trustful of, loyal to, or even affectionate towards them (Stines 2015). They will justify, side with, and defend the abuser, and will feel guilty and accept responsibility for their own mistreatment. They often blame themselves for the cruelty inflicted upon them. Trauma bonding occurs over time through the use of "intermittent reinforcement," a type of conditioning where a reward (or a punishment) is given irregularly instead of every time a desired behavior is observed. In other words, periods of cruelty are interspersed with periods of kindness (or absence of cruelty). This cycle keeps the target "on their toes" and in survival mode. They never know when the abuser will be cruel or kind. It's like a game of chance, like playing slot machines or Bingo. Sometimes you win, and sometimes you lose. It's the possibility of winning that keeps you going back for more.

With maternal narcissism, trauma bonds are created in several ways:

- Love bombing: The love bombing dynamic occurs when a narcissist mother unexpectedly showers her child with love, attention, kindness, or affection. Love bombing comes in various forms—gift-giving, forgiveness for past "offenses," going on a special outing, anything that makes the child feel validated or special. Love bombing helps form a trauma bond because it's a form of intermittent reinforcement: the child never knows when it will happen.

- Verbal abuse: Shouting, name-calling, sarcastic comments, character assassination, backhanded compliments, insults, demeaning remarks, "put-downs" and shaming are some examples of verbal abuse. It happens on an irregular schedule, so it's a form of intermittent reinforcement, spoken cruelty interspersed with periods of civility and kindness. The resulting shame causes a trauma bond.

- Positive reinforcement: Although it sounds healthy, positive reinforcement can also create trauma bonds. When a child is rewarded for doing something they didn't want to do, or obeying without question, there's a trauma bond created. Healthy relationships don't require rewards.

- Victim blaming: When a narcissist mother blames her child for the cruelty she inflicts on them, the child believes they deserve it, thus establishing a trauma bond.

- The silent treatment: When a narcissist mother ignores her child, that child feels helpless, anxious, and afraid they've been abandoned. Having no control over the situation, they'll focus on their mother and wait for her acceptance, however long it takes.

- "Moving goalposts" (aka changing the goal): Narcissist mothers often redefine or change their expectations, sometimes several times, during any interaction. This ensures a frustrating encounter for those involved. A narcissistic mother is never satisfied, and keeping her child emotionally invested in her happiness creates trauma bonds.

It's plain to see that any behavior that keeps you on high alert or focused on your mother is capable of forming trauma bonds. As we've seen, being on high alert, in survival mode, for any length of time can be harmful, and impact our ability to learn and remember.

Trauma bonds created with a narcissistic mother make future trauma bonding with other narcissists not only possible but likely. It feels natural to be in a relationship with a narcissistic person if you've been in one as a child (Firtel 2019).

After a trauma bond has developed, you may begin negatively perceiving anyone who tries to help you, and you may actually resent them for trying. When we're in a trauma bond with a narcissistic mother, we begin accepting the blame for her hurtful behavior and feel guilty because we think we caused it. We make excuses for her conduct, so our relationship appears "normal" to others.

Your intense, illogical loyalty and over-responsibility could continue in future relationships with other narcissists or abusive people if you don't become aware of your thoughts and actions. (Carnes and Phillips 2019).

HOW TO KNOW IF YOU'RE TRAUMA BONDED

These are some indicators that you're trauma bonded with someone:

- You think or fantasize a lot about a person who's hurt you

- You pursue contact with someone who's hurt you and could hurt you again

- You go out of your way to help someone who's hurt you

- You attempt to get people to like you when you know they're using you

- You repeatedly trust people whom you know are not trustworthy

- You don't leave unhealthy relationships

- You feel the need to be understood by people who don't want to understand

- You remain in a conflict instead of walking away

- You're loyal to someone who hurt or betrayed you

- You're attracted to people who need "fixing"

- You keep your history as a target of abuse a secret

- You stay in contact with a previous abuser

BREAK THE CHAINS

To break free from my trauma bonds, I practiced self-awareness and learned how to live in the moment, one day at a time. I built a network of emotionally stable friends and let go of those who weren't. I prioritized self-care.

If you haven't healed from the effects of maternal narcissism and you enter into a romantic relationship with a narcissist, you can assume it'll be full of drama and problems. You may discover that your new love interest has continued a physical relationship with their ex. Or you may notice yourself pretending that hurtful comments don't bother you. You might start putting up with or make excuses for their immature or inappropriate behavior, and you might even go along with requests you're uncomfortable with, just to keep his or her affection. Sometimes you'll give up personal or professional goals, friends, or activities, or deny your needs just to please or placate the new love interest. It may surprise you to know that you probably won't be aware of what you're doing. Many of the dynamics in the new relationship will be the same as those you have with your narcissistic mother. They'll feel familiar, and you'll know your role and what the expectations are.

In a healthy relationship, there is no trauma bonding. When a relationship is wholesome, no one makes excuses for the other's problematic behavior or poor choices. In fact, neither person feels responsible for making the other's choices or decisions or for the consequences thereof.

When we're free of codependent thinking and coping, we understand that we're separate and complete beings, whether involved in a romantic relationship or not. We have a strong sense of self and healthy boundaries in place. We feel comfortable setting new boundaries that keep us healthy, happy, and safe. We don't feel any need to justify, explain, or make sense of another person's behavior, to ourselves or anyone else. We understand that their choices and actions are their responsibility, not ours.

When we're in a healthy relationship, we don't feel any obligation or responsibility to help our partner avoid naturally occurring consequences. Instead, both parties understand that outcomes should be experienced by the person who's responsible for causing them. We realize that people learn by making mistakes. How will they learn to make different choices if we take the learning opportunity away from them? They won't.

> *"Every choice carries a consequence. For better or worse, each choice is the unavoidable consequence of its predecessor. There are not exceptions. If you can accept that a bad choice carries the seed of its own punishment, why not accept the fact that a good choice yields desirable fruit?"*
>
> –Gary Ryan Blair.

ACE's High

There's a lot of discussion in the field of education today about ACEs, "Adverse Childhood Experiences." ACEs are traumatic events that occur during childhood before age eighteen.

Childhood trauma research conducted in the 1990s discovered a connection between the number of ACEs a child experiences and the number of negative outcomes they experience in adulthood. These negative outcomes include health and medical issues, mental illness, addiction, and risk-taking behaviors. The original ACE Study was conducted from 1995 to 1997 at Kaiser Permanente. There were two waves of data collection from over seventeen thousand HMO members. The study concluded that experiencing a traumatic childhood significantly increases the probability that the child will suffer from future health issues, and adult-victimization as well.

When educators can understand childhood trauma's impact, trauma-informed interventions can be developed, which may reduce the number of negative consequences. Communities have also become involved in decreasing ACEs with prevention campaigns, which increase the number of positive outcomes for children and their families (Adverse Childhood Experiences, 2019).

Adverse Childhood Experiences are environmental influences that challenge a child's sense of safety, stability, and attachment. They include but are not limited to physical and verbal abuse, neglect, addiction, alcoholism, mental illness, and violence.

The ACE quiz is a data collection questionnaire that measures ten types of childhood trauma, five of which are personal: physical, verbal, and sexual abuse, and physical or emotional neglect. The remaining five are related to family members: an alcoholic parent, family member affected by domestic violence, incarcerated family member, mentally ill family member, or living in a single-parent household due to divorce, death, or abandonment. While there are many kinds of childhood trauma, only ten are included in the ACE quiz because they were the most frequently mentioned by the members of the research group. If other types of abuse or neglect were experienced, including extended periods of toxic stress, those would also increase the likelihood of compromised health in adulthood.

Each kind of traumatic experience scores one point. For example, a person who's been verbally abused and has a mentally ill parent, and lives in a single-parent home has an ACE score of three. The quiz is scored by adding all of the indicators. The harsher the childhood, the higher the score, and the higher the risk for problems in adulthood, such as risk-taking, chronic health conditions, mental illness, substance abuse, decreased or limited life-potential, and early death (Adverse Childhood Experiences 2019).

The ACE score is only a guideline. Positive childhood experiences can actually protect against many of the adverse outcomes, even after the trauma has occurred (Centers for Disease Control and Prevention, *About the CDC-Kaiser ACE study: Major findings*, 2016). Some people who have high ACE scores, including myself, can recover and do well as adults. Resilience, the subject of ongoing research, is considered a key component to recovery.

If you're interested in knowing your ACE score, take the Adverse Childhood Experiences quiz at https://www.stresshealth.org/ace-quiz/.

The first step to breaking trauma bonds is becoming aware that they exist. Trauma bonding can keep us stuck in codependency.

It's important to understand that Gaslighting, cognitive dissonance, and trauma bonding all contribute to developing a disorder called Complex Post Traumatic Stress Syndrome. We'll discuss that in more depth in a later chapter.

TAKEAWAYS

- Trauma bonding is a survival tool where the abused becomes emotionally attached to the abuser and will justify, side with, and defend them.

- Trauma bonding with a narcissistic mother makes future trauma bonding likely.

- In a healthy relationship, there is no trauma bonding.

- Trauma bonding can keep us stuck in codependency. The first step to breaking a trauma bond is becoming aware that one exists.

- "Adverse Childhood Experiences" include environmental factors that undermine a child's sense of safety, stability, and attachment. There is a connection between the number of ACEs a person experiences and health issues as an adult.

- The tool for determining these adverse adult outcomes is the ACE quiz.

ACTION FOR HEALING

1. To start breaking a trauma bond, you first need to admit that one exists. Think about the trauma bond symptoms. Have you experienced one? Are you in one now?

2. If you haven't already, read about mindfulness and learn how to start practicing it. Learning to be mindful and self-aware every

day will help you heal trauma bonds, codependency, your emotional triggers, and will help you see where your boundaries need to be. Mindfulness is one of the keys to healing.

3. Learn about negative self-talk, how to recognize it, and positively reframe it. Changing your self-talk is a major key to healing.

4. Make a list of everything that you will not miss about your trauma bond after it's dissolved

5. Have you taken the ACE test? What's your score? What does this indicate to you? How do you feel about it?

Chapter Fifteen
SLAMMING AND BANGING

"The more you love yourself, the less nonsense you'll tolerate."

—Unknown

Because narcissists are opinionated, argumentative, and defensive, they have no problem confronting, criticizing, or mocking anyone who challenges or disagrees with them. Narcissists don't entertain differences of opinion or perspectives. Instead, they gaslight, humiliate, insult, discredit, or have a meltdown known as narcissistic rage. These rages happen when we do anything that causes a narcissistic injury.

NARCISSISTIC RAGES

Narcissistic anger and rage are similar to an adult temper tantrum, except they're not cute and are more dangerous. Episodes consist of unexpected and uncontrollable outrage triggered by some type of narcissistic injury. For example, if their self-esteem or self-worth has been wounded, a rage will probably ensue.

When they're caught up in an angry outburst, narcissists are unreasonable and vengeful. Their objective is revenge. They want to win the argument and punish the offender, even if it means losing a relationship or irrevocably damaging one. They won't feel regret, remorse, or any need to apologize for their volatile, hurtful, or attention-seeking eruption.

Narcissistic rages are fear-based and persist even *after* the threat is gone. Often, narcissistic rages are not warranted, but if there is a justifiable reason, a narcissistic mom will hang onto the memory of that transgression for weeks and months at a time. Narcissists are champion grudge holders because grudges vindicate their behavior and give them a reason to feel victimized. A narcissist-mom will bring up wrongdoing as frequently as she can, playing the "poor me" to get sympathy and supply.

WHY THEY RAGE

"Slamming and banging" is a type of narcissistic rage and a scenario I regularly experienced while growing up. When my mother was angry or couldn't express her feelings, she would slam and bang things—usually, cupboard doors, car doors, bedroom doors, but it could be any object within reach. This was the way she demonstrated she was annoyed, disappointed, insulted, angry, or frustrated. She didn't use words to express feelings unless they were shouted, hurtful, and inappropriate.

When I was young and too naive to appreciate the danger of doing so, if I asked, during an episode of slamming and banging, "Is something wrong, Mommy?" She typically snapped "No," which was another of her confusing mixed messages. Something *was* wrong, and even a child could see that. If I kept pressing, I paid the price by getting shouted at, called hurtful names, humiliated, or shamed. It was not good to ask questions, even as an act of kindness or concern.

As I got older, my question changed from "Is there something wrong?" to "What's wrong?" I knew I wasn't going to continue playing "let's pretend." I could see that there was clearly something bothering her, and I called her out. If you live in a dysfunctional family, you understand that "reality" is never "real" because everyone in the family plays, "let's pretend." But everyone's pretending something different.

Passive Aggressive Rage

Sometimes narcissistic rages don't actually look like rages. They're passive-aggressive, and they can involve sulking, giving backhanded compliments, procrastinating, sarcastic remarks, withdrawal, sabotaging and undermining, and even the silent treatment. These methods are all subtle and discreet, but they're narcissistic rages nonetheless. My mother vacillated between intimidating furies and passive aggression. At times she shouted, hurling obscenities so loudly and fiercely that she'd turn purple. Her eyes bulged, her lips curled as if snarling, spittle flying. It was terrifying to see her like that, not only because she looked frightening, but because she was emotionally out of control. At these times, I never knew what to expect, so I was on high alert and prepared for anything. I might be backhanded across the face or hauled into a bedroom and left, or ignored for hours. I might be called names that shredded my character and crushed my spirit. I might have my dinner beverage dumped over my head. I could be deprived of meals or activities, or threatened with abandonment. Or she could simply and completely withdraw from my life, not speaking to me.

What Triggers a Rage?

More than four decades after their divorce, I learned that my mother routinely called the Social Security Administration to confirm that my father was still alive. She was motivated by a firm determination to receive survivor benefits when he passed.

One morning, she made the usual call and discovered that my father had passed away six months prior. She called me at work to tell me that my father was dead, and she was livid that no one had contacted her, outraged that she'd missed out on several months of financial benefits. She was extremely distraught and asked me to come over after I finished my workday.

When I got there, she wanted me to drive her to the post office. I found that she'd written a letter to my father's widow, his wife of more than forty years, and she wanted to send it by certified mail. She knew the address because she'd openly stalked my father for years. When I warily asked about the letter's contents, I learned that it was a scathing chastisement for not informing my mother, or the family, of his death. I didn't take her, and I don't know if the letter was ever sent.

"Your mother's narcissistic rages have nothing to do with you. Narcissism is a mental illness caused by events on which you had no influence".

This day-long narcissistic rage was triggered by the huge sense of injustice and entitlement that my mother felt. She had been "wronged"; she had been slighted. She had been overlooked as the first wife. She had been denied her rightful due; all narcissistic injuries. Later the same day, I discovered that within hours of the news of his death, she began busily informing family members and her community that she'd become a "widow," readily accepting condolences and sympathy. The rage had passed; she was a victim once again.

Here are some other ways that narcissistic injuries can trigger rage in a narcissistic mom:

- Someone criticized her.

- She was not the center of attention.

- She was embarrassed.

- She was confronted.

- Someone pointed out a character flaw.

- Someone noticed that she'd made an error.

- She was caught lying, cheating, stealing, or breaking a rule of acceptable behavior.

- She felt like she was losing control.

- Her authority was challenged or threatened.

- Someone made a decision without her input.

- Someone took the initiative without her permission.

- Someone was appreciated (or more highly regarded) than she.

- Someone didn't take her advice.

- She was asked to be accountable for her actions.

- She did not get the special treatment she thought she deserved.

- She was reminded of her inadequacy.

- She was shamed.

THE CONSEQUENCES OF RAGE

Narcissists may pay a heavy price for their rages.

Preston Ni (2018), in "Understanding Narcissism's Destructive Impact on Relationships," talks about the possible consequences a narcissist may suffer as a result of ongoing, vindictive, narcissistic anger.

- *Family Estrangement:* Research shows that narcissistic rages hurt family relationships.

- *Lost romantic relationships and divorce:* Research shows that rages hurt romantic relationships and marriages.

- *Isolation:* Narcissists use people for personal gain. Eventually, acquaintances, family, and friends recognize this and distance themselves or go "no contact."

- *Loneliness:* Narcissists have few healthy or lasting relationships.

- *Missed Opportunities:* Because of the lack of personal connection, opportunities may disappear or don't appear in the first place.

- *Legal, Financial, or Career issues:* Rule-breaking, irresponsibility, and carelessness are found to have legal and financial repercussions.

- *Damaged Reputation:* A lack of personal or professional integrity, trustworthiness, or dependability can negatively impact others' perceptions.

HOW TO HANDLE NARCISSISTIC RAGES

You can take several actions to protect yourself during a rage:

- Set boundaries

- Limit the amount of contact

- Don't engage. Walk away

- Use the Gray Rock technique, explained in the "Talking with Your Mother" chapter

- Use the communication strategies outlined in the "Talking with Your Mother" chapter

- Talk to a mental health professional or therapist

Understand that a narcissistic rage has nothing to do with you. Narcissism is a mental illness caused by events that you did not influence. You didn't cause the narcissism, you can't control it, and you can't cure it. You *can* control how you respond to it.

Takeaways

- Narcissistic rage consists of unexpected and uncontrollable anger triggered by some type of narcissistic injury. For example, self-esteem or self-worth having been jeopardized or wounded.

- Holding a grudge vindicates a narcissist mother's behavior and gives her reason to feel victimized.

- Sometimes rages are passive-aggressive; for example, sulking, giving backhanded compliments, procrastination, making sarcastic comments, withdrawal, sabotage, undermining, and using the silent treatment.

Action for Healing

1. You've seen the list of triggers that could result in your mother experiencing a narcissistic rage. Write examples of the tantrums you've been subjected to.

2. Write about how you handled these rages. How did they make you feel?

3. Develop a list of actions you can take to protect yourself from or avoid a narcissistic rage.

4. In the past, how did you handle rages? How will you handle future rages?

Chapter Sixteen
GASLIGHTING: THE MOST SIGNIFICANT CAUSE OF C-PTSD

"Because of its insidious nature, gaslighting is one form of emotional abuse that is hard to recognize and even more challenging to break free from. Part of that is because the narcissist exploits one of our greatest fears—the fear of being alone."

–Angie Atkinson

Even though I held a psychology degree and enjoyed paid-experience as a mental health professional, I was reluctant to "label" my mother. My continued unwillingness to identify the problem was partly due to my codependency and our trauma bond.

After I had the revelation with my therapist about my mom's probable personality disorder, I was finally able to drop the fantasy that someday we'd have a "normal," happy, mother/daughter relationship, and I started educating myself about narcissism.

The new information and validation strongly impacted me. I was grateful that it came at a time during which I was exhausted from being her narcissistic-supply. I was her Emotional Care-Taker, Head-Cheerleader, Chief-Validator, Affirmation-Support-Specialist, and CEO of her "Poor Me" department.

I was mentally and emotionally drained from keeping up the charade that I was fine, while actively lying to and gaslighting myself. Self-deception takes SOOOO much energy! I decided to drop *all of it* and just get REAL with myself.

SOWING SEEDS OF DOUBT

As I've mentioned before, "gaslighting" is a term borrowed from the 1938 stage play *Gaslight*. In this tale, a husband attempts to drive his wife insane by dimming their home's gas-powered lights and then denying it when his wife notices. This ploy causes her to doubt her perception, judgment, memory, and reality. She begins to believe she's losing her mind.

Narcissist moms intentionally gaslight their kids to obtain some narcissistic supply. Gaslighting is emotional abuse in the form of mind games; the ability to control our beliefs, feelings, thoughts, perceptions, actions, and reactions provides them with instant and ongoing narcissistic supply.

A narcissist mom typically remains calm and rational after gaslighting her child, which, by contrast, can make them feel insecure and irrational.

When you're being gaslighted, especially if you're a child, you don't know what's happening, but you intuitively know that you're involved in "something" your mother is intentionally doing. You can't figure out what it is or why she's doing it. You're primarily confused, stressed, and frustrated, and you can't figure out the reason for it. (Atkinson, Angela). Gaslighting gives a narcissist mother a great deal of power and control.

You're likely being gaslighted if:

- Your narcissistic mother uses your fears or insecurities against you. If you divulge personal worries to her, at some point, they will be used as weapons against you.

- Your mother wants you to think she knows you better than you know yourself. Sometimes, she might say she knows what you're thinking. If you tell her she's wrong, she'll believe you're lying. She may roll her eyes or make a disgusted face. Narcissists simply cannot allow themselves to be wrong. She'd rather believe you're a liar than admit she's incorrect.

- Your mom expects you to do things that may not be appropriate, ethical, or legal.

- If you're regularly told that something's customary or OK when you know it isn't, then you're probably being gaslighted. For example, my mother frequently forced me to lie on the phone, or at the door, to other adult family or friends on her behalf. Usually, the lie was something minor like that she had a headache, or was in bed, sick, or wasn't home. Growing up this way, I believed that lying for one's mother was expected and a reasonable thing to do. In my teens, I began recognizing that this wasn't something all kids had to do, and I refused to continue. I had the feeling I was being used. I also believed that she should, as an adult, speak for herself. She was disgusted with me for expecting her to be honest or to do her own lying.

- Your mother "diagnoses" you and tells you what's wrong with you. You're informed that you're mentally ill or that you have "issues." When a narcissist doesn't get their way, they'll insult you and question your judgment or your sanity. They may tell you that you need therapy or medication. This really isn't about you, though. It's about her need to feel superior and control you and the relationship.

- Your mother rewrites history. She informs you that what you know to be accurate or real is, in fact, not correct or factual. The most common type of gaslighting I experienced was when I witnessed my mother saying or doing something frightening, threatening, mean-spirited (basically when she was exhibiting a narcissistic rage). I'd ask her about it, and she'd gaslight me. For example, once while visiting, I overheard her verbally abuse my invalid grandmother. Mother was loud and angry, swearing, cursing, name-calling, and throwing obscenities. I confronted her when she left the bedroom. She hadn't known I was there and looked shocked to see me. Then, acting insulted, she said, "What are you talking about? I never did that."

She regularly and consistently denied saying or doing anything that would harm her image.

- Your mother insists that your memory is unreliable. Narcissistic mothers often recall or retell events very differently than you remember them. She describes her behavior or reactions as rational, but often spins yours as irrational or shameful.

Don't try to convince yourself that events in your childhood didn't happen the way you remember them. Don't gaslight yourself, my friend. You've had enough of that already. Be honest with yourself, even if it's scary.

SELF-GASLIGHTING: CARRYING ON THE TRADITION

Do you gaslight yourself? I use the term "self-gaslighting" to describe the activity of minimizing or invalidating your mother's hurtful behavior. Examples are: making excuses for her behavior, convincing yourself that an event didn't happen (or that it didn't happen the way you remember it), or accepting her rewritten versions of past events even though they conflict with your memories.

Self-gaslighting is a form of doubt that contributes to cognitive dissonance.

When we self-gaslight, we may tell ourselves that our mother's choice or behavior was our fault. Or we may convince ourselves that we somehow provoked her hurtful behavior. We might take responsibility for the choices she made and the things she did that hurt us. We not only *accept* blame, but we intentionally place it on ourselves. Isn't that *amazing?* We lie to ourselves and then spend precious emotional energy, convincing ourselves that we're *not.* It's crazy-making and exhausting, and it's time to stop.

Enough.

"Self-gaslighting results from being a target of persistent gaslighting and remaining in cognitive dissonance."

When you try to convince yourself that you didn't just hear what you know you heard or that you didn't just see what you know you saw….you are self-gaslighting. Become aware that you're doing it and *stop* every time. Remind yourself that you're not doing that anymore, that you're honest with yourself now. Stand up for yourself and become your own advocate. If you won't, then who will? Tell yourself the truth and stop accepting gaslighting from anybody, *including yourself*, period.

Cognitive dissonance is a type of mental stress that results from struggling to correct the surreal-gap between what we *know* is real, and what we are *told* is real. It is *the* crazy-making component of gaslighting. We can't continue living in that state of confusion, not knowing what to believe and what not to believe, and not knowing whether we can rely on our feelings, judgment, or senses. Our natural state of "being" *requires* that our thoughts and interactions make sense to us. When we feel doubtful of our reality or are so fearful of making a decision that we're emotionally paralyzed, it may be the result of gaslighting's cognitive dissonance.

When we're gaslighted regularly, our level of cognitive dissonance grows, and the crazier and more out-of-touch we feel. We're unsure of what's real and what's not, what's true and what's not, and we don't know whether to believe our senses or only to accept what we're *told*.

We *all* tell ourselves stories. It's how we make sense of ourselves and the world. Our ego translates our experiences, so they make sense, and it can keep us stuck in a loop of revisiting confusing memories. Rather than remain stuck, we accept the best explanation. Think about the possible explanations a six-year-old might create, versus a twenty-year-old, or a thirty-five-year-old. Age and immaturity work against us when we're abused as kids because we're not experienced or knowledgeable enough to imagine plausible and realistic explanations.

At four, if my mother ignores me, I might think it's because she doesn't love me. And if I'm ignored throughout my childhood, I may come to interpret it as "I'm unlovable," and carry that belief forward into adulthood. But at thirty, if my mother ignores me, I might think it's because she's preoccupied, tired, not feeling well, etc. I can choose any number of explanations, and they'll align with my current self-concept. For example, if I believe I'm unlovable, my interpretation of other's behavior will reflect that belief. If I have strong self-esteem, then my interpretation will reflect that. We interpret our reality through these emotional "filters." It's important to remember this because our filters can and do change. Our perceptions and interpretations continually change and develop as we mature physically, intellectually, socially, spiritually, and emotionally. This is one of the biggest reasons for doing the healing-work of *examining our beliefs* and trashing the ones that don't apply (or aren't relevant) anymore.

Remember that beliefs are thoughts that have emotions attached to them. Eliminating inaccurate beliefs is a primary key to healing. Pick one of your childhood beliefs to examine. What thoughts and feelings are still connected to it? For example: "I won't ever be successful." List the feelings and thoughts that come up and write about them at length. Are they still relevant to your life today? Why or why not? Explain. Learn about therapeutic approaches like Tapping, Neurolinguistic Programming, or Cognitive Behavioral Therapy to create healthy new beliefs about yourself. Investigate other ways of changing your beliefs.

We acquired our beliefs as children. We get to replace them as adults.

AM I CRAZY?

Gaslighting can have severe consequences, especially if it's ongoing. If you're being gaslighted, you may begin lying to avoid stress, arguments, or prevent your mother from becoming triggered, angry, or abusive. You'll also want to control outcomes because of the sense of predictability or stability it offers.

For those of us who've been gaslighted, it's one of our most challenging aspects of healing because we've learned to disregard our perception, self-trust, judgment, and our ability to remember. Because we may have learned to trust our mother's interpretation of the world and events, we may begin to rely on her judgment and perception instead of our own.

When you've been gaslighted, you probably got unexpected or inappropriate responses to common questions or actions. Your own reactions may have been determined to be incorrect, unreasonable, or shameful. You may wonder why your mother gives you strange looks that cause you to question your every action or word. Fearful for your mental health, you worry that you're losing your mind. You accept that you're the illogical one, or that you're mentally ill. You're confused by things she says and does, but your observations can't be validated because you're often the only witness.

I'd often get confused, stressed, and frustrated when my mother denied doing something I'd just witnessed. I'd ask, "You're saying that I didn't see what I know I just saw?" And she'd reply in an exasperated or dismayed tone of voice, "You dreamt it," "You imagined it," or "So-and-so did that, not me." Hhmmm.

COGNITIVE DISSONANCE: GASLIGHTING'S UGLY COUSIN

As targets of gaslighting, we may become so confounded that we stop trusting our intuition and our senses. This gives a narcissistic mother considerable advantages (Newman, S. 2018).

Humans have a natural need for their attitudes, beliefs, and behaviors to exist amicably with each other. This is known as "cognitive consistency," and living in a state of cognitive consistency means that we feel stable, relaxed, and at peace with our daily choices. For example, if I believe I'm an honest person, and I act accordingly, it means I'll tell the truth even when it's uncomfortable or gets me into trouble. I'll maintain my integrity and cognitive consistency.

On the flip side, cognitive *dissonance* indicates a state of opposing viewpoints, beliefs, or behaviors. Although it sounds negative, cognitive dissonance can be healthy. It causes us to question ourselves and motivates us to resolve inconsistencies between our actions and beliefs. This keeps us mentally balanced and encourages us toward new levels of personal growth. But when cognitive dissonance is unhealthy, it's usually a result of manipulation. To restore emotional balance, the afflicted person must change or remove the inconsistency or conflict.

For those of us who've experienced gaslighting, it causes harmful cognitive dissonance and reduces us to confused, uncertain, dependent shadows of our former selves. It robs us of our ability to think, make decisions, and use sound judgment. We wind up doubting ourselves and fear we're losing our minds. I believe that gaslighting is the most treacherous form of manipulation because it undermines our sense of self and reality.

"It all begins and ends in your mind. What you give power to has power over you, if you allow it."

—Leon Brown

Most of us consciously or unconsciously resolve cognitive dissonance by doing one of these three things:

1. Change our thoughts: Choosing this option means you change your thoughts and beliefs to match those of your narcissistic mom. For example, you accept your mother's perspective that you lack common sense, rather than continue believing that you have sound judgment. Now you agree with your mother, which eliminates the emotional conflict and cognitive dissonance.

2. Change our actions: With this approach, you change your behavior, so it matches your beliefs about yourself. Using the above example, you find ways to demonstrate that you *actually*

have sound judgment and common sense. Your actions now match your mindset, eliminating the emotional conflict and cognitive dissonance.

3. Justify our perceptions: You really do lack common sense and sound judgment, and you rationalize this by minimizing their value and significance. In essence, you trivialize your lack of common sense and sound judgment to eliminate the emotional conflict and cognitive dissonance.

Resolving cognitive dissonance isn't always done on a conscious level, although we may be aware that we have some choices to make. At some point, we'll use one of these three methods to keep our sanity and self-esteem.

But eliminating cognitive dissonance isn't a "one and done" kind of thing. Typically, and speaking from my own experience, we play around with the three possibilities for resolution, trying them on, seeing how they fit and feel. Eventually, we settle on one that suits us best: one that our mother will accept, and that causes us the least mental stress.

Because my mother liked to overwrite my perceptions and memories with her own, I heard a lot of, "I never said that," "You imagined it," "You dreamt it," or "It wasn't me." I was in a continual state of self-doubt and confusion from her insistence that I perceived and remembered events inaccurately. My ability to make decisions and to trust my own senses was severely negatively impacted. I eventually came to believe that the discrepancies between my own observations and those of my mother were flaws in my memory and perception. I became obsessed with explaining the disparities between what I observed and what I was told I observed. I remained in a state of cognitive dissonance throughout my childhood.

EFFECTS OF GASLIGHTING

This form of abuse often leads to feeling depressed, anxious, helpless, hopeless, or exhausted. If it's severe, you may feel like your sense of self is "fuzzy" and "reality" feels dreamlike. You probably can't think clearly and have trouble with problem solving and making decisions.

And while you're struggling, your narcissistic mother will continue to play these mind games, twisting your memories and experiences.

Eventually, you may begin to depend on your mother to tell you what's real and what isn't. You'll rely on her to tell you what you've experienced and how you remember it. If gaslighting is constant, your understanding of reality may eventually depend on your mother's interpretation. You'll begin to lose your sense of self, and you may start to dissociate. Dissociation happens when you feel disconnected from your sensory input, your sense of self, or personal experiences. It feels like you're losing your sense of who you are, what you're doing, or where you are.

COGNITIVE DISTORTIONS

An interesting topic that's related to cognitive dissonance is that of "cognitive distortions."

As you can imagine, when someone has spent a lot of time in an unsafe-feeling environment, it can cause them to see the world a bit differently than their peers. Without treatment or intervention, "reality" feels somewhat exaggerated, intense, discouraging, and even threatening. Because those affected tend to look for justification for their adverse worldview, every miscommunication or misunderstanding feels like it could be a personal attack. These faulty thoughts are called "cognitive distortions." Cognitive distortions are a twisted and harmful way of reasoning, intentionally misrepresenting reality and spinning experiences into something other than what they are. This practice validates and maintains a negative view of life.

Social psychologist, Dr. Alice Boyes, has aggregated a list of fifty common cognitive distortions. Here are a few of them:

- **Overgeneralizing:** Applying the result of one isolated event to other areas of life.

- **"All or nothing" thinking:** Also known as black and white thinking, a limited viewpoint that doesn't allow any "gray" areas.

- **Negativity bias:** Only noticing the negative aspects of life and not the positives.

- **Catastrophizing:** Anticipating the worst in every situation or anticipating arbitrary or bizarre consequences that probably won't happen.

- **Double standards for yourself:** Everything you do has to be perfect, or it's not acceptable.

- **Jumping to conclusions:** Assuming to know what other people will say, do, or think—and that it will be negative.

- **Taking everything personally:** Seeing a personal attack in any disagreeable interaction (Boyes 2013).

If you notice yourself using cognitive distortions, it's crucial to practice self-awareness to correct it.

Look for and recognize these errors in thinking as they occur. Make a note of them in your journal. Why do you think you've used the specific distortions that you have?

Replace them with other, healthy thoughts. A trusted counselor, coach, or friend can help you spot faulty thinking and replace it.

TAKEAWAYS

- Gaslighting is a type of emotional abuse that's hard to recognize and challenging to heal.

- Gaslighting gives a narcissist a considerable amount of power and control. It's emotional abuse in the form of mind games. When narcissists gaslight, they feel superior in their control over your beliefs, feelings, thoughts, and perceptions.

- If you're frequently gaslighted, you may doubt your reality or your memory. You may convince yourself that your mother's version of reality is accurate.

- If the gaslighting is constant, your sense of reality may eventually depend on your mother's interpretation. You may begin to lose your sense of self.

- Humans have a natural need to live in cognitive consistency so we can feel stable, secure, and peaceful about ourselves and our choices.

- There are three ways we can eliminate cognitive dissonance: change our thoughts, change our actions, or justify our perceptions.

- Cognitive distortions are errors in thinking. They're a way to spin life experiences into something different than what they are, in effect, validating and maintaining a negative view of life.

Action for Healing

1. Start letting go. It's time to stop focusing on your mother's narcissistic behavior and start moving forward into a new way of experiencing life. It's time to start adjusting your attitude and putting yourself on your own "to-do" list as a priority. Make a conscious decision to move forward.

2. Develop your self-confidence. Get into counseling, take a class, learn a new skill, start a hobby. Reclaim your personal power and self-esteem.

3. Practice mindfulness, and be fully present in the moment. Let go of worry, stress, and anxiety, and focus on what's happening *now*. You'll begin to notice a new sense of trust and even peace.

4. Start building new, healthy relationships, and connect to others in new ways. Doing these will help you attract better relationships and authentic, supportive friends.

5. Gaslighting erodes your trust in yourself, so it's essential to give yourself permission to make mistakes and learn from them. Life is about attaining progress, not perfection. Remember, you're a human being. No one is perfect, regardless of what your mother may insist on.

6. Find ways to affirm your choices so you'll start trusting your judgment and decision-making ability.

7. Make notes or checklists, whatever works for you, as a way of affirming your observations and your memories. It's time to regain your life. It doesn't happen quickly, but each day that you do the necessary recovery work will make a difference.

8. Continue actively exploring how your childhood and identity might have been affected by gaslighting.

9. Write about any gaslighting episodes you remember. Write how the incident occurred as you remember it, and then write how it was rewritten by your mother. Find someone who was present during the original event and see how their memory of what happened compares to yours. Seek validation that your memories are accurate

Chapter Seventeen
CODEPENDENCY

"We repeat what we don't repair."

–Christine Langley-Obaugh

If we grow up in an environment that lacks nurturing, and we take care of or focus on ourselves, we eventually get a clear message from our family members that we're self-centered or selfish. Sooner or later, we may begin ignoring our self-care because "selfish" doesn't align with our self-concept of "helper, fixer, do-er." So, we may begin negatively judging ourselves for doing those things that we enjoy, and we may stop doing them. We may eventually cease taking care of ourselves and start focusing on others. Everyone else becomes our priority.

We may even regard this self-sacrificing behavior as positive. For me, being helpful meant rushing to aid anyone who was struggling. It meant cleaning up their messes (literally and figuratively) and getting between them and their due consequences. I thought this was an excellent way to show how much I cared, but in effect, it actually made it easier for them to continue making poor choices. I needed to address my "helping" behavior, my "need to be needed," and my belief that "fixing and controlling" made me a good person. But I wasn't ready to challenge myself about those until much later.

Someone once pointed out that in doing these "helpful" things, I might be interfering with karma or with intended life lessons. Whaaaat? I was intrigued and horrified. Was I really doing that? Who was I to interfere with anyone's spiritual and personal growth or life lessons? Surely this wasn't the case. I was such a supportive and caring person! How could "caring" and "helping" do any harm?

Slacking on my responsibilities, so that I could take on ones that didn't belong to me, seemed selfless and helpful. Fixing circumstances, giving unsolicited advice, and taking over problems when I wasn't asked to, made me feel good about myself. I felt empathetic, compassionate, and willing to get involved and make a difference. But I was actually doing a disservice. I was acting from a place of "empathy on crack," as I've heard codependency described. *Was I codependent?* With time and introspection, I began to see that "helping" was for my own self-esteem and ego-gratification. I was acting from a deep-seated need to be needed.

"Not my circus, not my clowns."

——Anonymous

WHAT IS CODEPENDENCY?

In his book "Codependency for Dummies," Dr. Charles Whitfield defines it as "a disease of a lost self."

In "Codependency, An Emerging Issue," Robert Subby says that it results from rules preventing "open expression" of feelings. (Pompano Beach, FL, Health Communications Inc.,1984, pp. 34-44)

Wow. I think those definitions are spot-on. That's exactly what it feels like for those of us who are codependent. Bit by bit, we cut off pieces of ourselves until we became someone else's idea of who we should be. There were times I wondered if there was ever an authentic "me" inside somewhere. When I got to adulthood, I didn't know my favorite food, or my favorite color, musician, book, movie, restaurant, sports team, or author. I didn't associate with a political party or have a favorite music genre. I had no career trajectory or life-goal. In short, I didn't know the details about myself that I knew about my mother and other people in my life. These are the results of an other-directed, other-focused upbringing.

When we're children who don't have mentally healthy role models and caregivers, we don't learn or develop healthy coping skills to equip ourselves in adulthood. Often, we simply imitate other family members' maladaptive coping methods, such as using manipulation, physical aggression, substances, or food, which do more harm than good. Codependency is a set of maladaptive coping skills.

If we became codependent as children, we were probably caretakers for our mothers, and possibly other adults and siblings. We were likely required to mature quickly and take responsibilities that were not age-appropriate. When it felt unsafe being around our mothers, we learned to tiptoe around her instability so as not to upset her. We learned to "put-up and shut-up." We monitored her moods and responded accordingly, we noticed behavioral patterns, and we became very good at predicting her behavior. We learned how to take the initiative in making her life easier or better so *we* could feel a sense of stability and safety. We became accustomed to doing things for others that they could do for themselves.

THE THREE STAGES OF CODEPENDENCY

Codependency exists on a continuum, from mild to severe, just as narcissism does. There are three stages in the development of codependency; the loss of self, a need to placate the abuser, and a need to control the consequences of the abuser's behavior. Let's talk about each of those:

Loss of self: This early-stage of codependency looks like paying an increasing amount of attention to your mother. You may monitor her moods, become hypervigilant, and feel a strong desire to please her. In this phase, we deny or rationalize her problem behaviors and fabricate explanations that maintain our sense of safety: "Mom had a bad day," or "Mom's just tired." We endure gaslighting because our focus is on keeping her calm and minimizing the attacks. We don't make waves.

Need to placate: This stage takes an increased effort to continue denying or minimizing the more painful aspects of our relationship with our mother. We likely feel anxious, guilty, and ashamed. We purposefully hide these feelings along with the problems that exist in our relationship. We may withdraw from other relationships and activities we enjoy. Our self-esteem decreases, and we continue to compromise ourselves in an effort to maintain a semblance of stability or predictability at home. Our focus is usually on our mothers, and taking her "emotional temperature" comes in handy. We learn to adjust our behavior and expectations according to what we sense is happening with her. We may feel angry, disappointed, unloved, or unimportant when we're in this phase of codependency. We may begin using maladaptive coping behaviors, which include but are not limited to eating, bingeing, self-harming, stealing, engaging in risky sexual activity, or abusing substances.

Need to control consequences: In late-stage codependency, the emotional and behavioral symptoms will start affecting us. We may start to experience health issues like stomachaches, nightmares, headaches, muscle pain, tension, and TMJ. Self-esteem and self-care are almost nonexistent at this point, replaced by feelings of hopelessness, helplessness, anger, resentment, and overall unhappiness.

Since kids are genuinely dependent upon their caretakers, codependency can't be diagnosed until they attain adulthood. It usually manifests with the beginning of close adult relationships.

Codependent adults often spend their time thinking about how to appease and make life better for their narcissistic mother, while their own social, professional, and personal responsibilities get neglected. They will continue focusing on their mothers despite the problems this creates. Because ACNs still desire connection, love, and affection from their mothers, they continue compromising themselves, emotionally caretaking her, chasing after her love and affection, and settling for crumbs.

Codependency eventually affects our ability to have healthy, mutually satisfying adult relationships. Because we feel confused, distrustful, hesitant, disoriented, and emotionally exhausted, we find ourselves searching for answers and explanations. Codependency is a set of learned behaviors that can be passed down through generations. It lends itself nicely to all kinds of unhealthy relationships because codependent relationships exhibit a lot of emotional drama. It wouldn't be unusual to find ourselves in relationships involving alcoholism, substance abuse, and mental illness, including narcissism.

ARE YOU CODEPENDENT?

To determine if you're using codependent behavior when you relate to your mother or others, answer the following questions:

1. Have you taken actions that prevent someone from feeling or experiencing the consequences of their choices?

    It feels like we're really helpful when we do that, but it's quite the opposite. Ask yourself: Am I trying to control what happens in this situation? If the answer's yes, you're likely using codependent behavior.

2. Do you take responsibility for someone else's actions or poor choices?

    When you take responsibility (or accept blame or make excuses) for someone's harmful or hurtful behavior, it "enables" them to keep doing it. (a) You've taken all the responsibility away from them and placed it on yourself, and (b) there are no negative consequences. No "lesson" has been learned because they've gotten away with their behavior. This cycle can happen repeatedly. It rewards irresponsibility and teaches a sense of entitlement.

3. Do you do things for adults that they could do for themselves?

    As codependent adults, we're what's known as "people pleasers." We need to be needed. To others, we codependents may appear as meddlesome busybodies. We may always seem to be involved in other people's business or with things that shouldn't concern us. Or we may appear to be unselfish, someone who can be counted on. Someone who never says "no."

Although it often feels right to take care of others, we're often left feeling taken advantage of or resentful. So, if you feel resentful about something you did or are doing for someone, it might be that you're using codependent behavior.

"Ending codependency is a state of mind. It involves no longer being willing to compromise yourself to earn affection, attention, acceptance, and validation. Your "people-pleasing" days are over."

Codependency includes behaviors like:

- Being preoccupied or concerned with the needs of others

- Placing a low priority on your own needs

- Being attracted to needy or emotionally unavailable people

- Believing that you have to be in a romantic relationship before you your life feels meaningful

- Trying to control another's behavior

- Feeling incapable of ending a harmful or toxic relationship

- Trying to please everyone even though you know you'll feel resentful

- Not taking time for yourself, or ignoring your self-care

- Fearing for another's safety but being willing to risk your safety

- Shielding someone from the consequences of their actions

- Taking responsibility for how another person feels

- Taking responsibility for what another person does

- Trying to fix someone's problem when they haven't asked you to

- Helping because it makes you feel better

- Feeling like your life is full of unwanted drama

Living as a codependent means that we're not going to get our needs met, yet asking for anything on our own behalf feels wrong, imposing, undeserved, or selfish.

Ask yourself if you have codependent behaviors.

1. Have I/do I try to manage or control someone else's life?

2. Have I taken on responsibilities that aren't mine?

3. Have I ever been called "controlling" or a "control freak?"

4. Do I take care of others by cleaning up their messes, both figuratively and otherwise?

5. Do I keep others from dealing with the consequences of their actions?

6. Do I do things for others that they can do for themselves?

How many of those behaviors do you engage in? Do you use codependent thinking and behavior? Keep going. Add more! Write as many as you can think of!

As codependents, we're afraid of dissatisfying others. If we disappoint anyone, it often leads to feeling guilt and shame, yet we continually look for someone to please. We make excuses for their poor behavior or mistreatment of us, and we minimize the pain they cause. Holding on to this mindset and behavior pattern will attract dysfunctional people to us.

There is a certain degree of cognitive dissonance experienced when accepting your own codependency. It helps if you're willing to take a pretty deep and fearless dive into what's actually going on. When I was ready, I began looking at how I chose to spend my time and noticing who was benefitting and who was not. I started to see it when I took care of other's needs and ignored or denied my own. I asked myself why I made the choices I did. Little by little, I learned to live in the moment with awareness and intention. My negative self-talk had once enforced my belief that everyone's needs should be addressed before my own. I started changing the self-talk and questioning the beliefs.

"Allow others the dignity and space to make and learn from their own mistakes."

Through therapy, support groups, reading, and listening to other recovering codependents, I learned a lot. I discovered that when people don't experience their own naturally occurring consequences, they often have a difficult time accepting responsibility, acquiring social skills, and developing the personal characteristics required for successful relationships. These include the ability to share, tell the truth, listen, negotiate, or compromise. If we shield others from experiencing naturally occurring adverse consequences, they won't learn how to shift their perspectives to see the bigger picture of how seemingly unrelated things are actually connected.

I'd always thought of myself as a helpful person. I liked that quality about myself. I often thought of and referred to myself as an "action taker" and a "do-er" rather than a "talker." I didn't realize then that this was a codependent mindset.

Some of the steps I took to break free of codependency were: using self-awareness, living in the moment, focusing on one day at a time, building a network of emotionally healthy friends, letting go of ones who weren't, and prioritizing self-care. I had to learn to let go of my desire to control outcomes, no matter how good my intentions were. I had to get comfortable watching loved ones deal with the results of their poor choices. I had to sit still and stay uninvolved when they made poor decisions, even if it hurt them or cost them money or relationships.

Setting boundaries, saying "no," and letting others learn their life lessons "the hard way" became my goals. I had to see my role in creating the trauma bonds, and I had to break those bonds. To try to do all of these simultaneously would have left me feeling intolerably guilty, irrelevant, and without self-esteem, not to mention exhausted. But I didn't learn or do them all at once. It was a slow, deliberate, and sometimes painful process.

Taking similar steps may help you too. Allow yourself to acknowledge and fully feel your emotions every day. Continue validating yourself. Catch yourself when you start to lie to or gaslight yourself—no more denial. Your life might not be great right now, but it's OK. You're about to change that.

Those of us who have experienced maternal narcissistic abuse may eventually find ourselves in abusive, toxic, or less-than-satisfying adult relationships. It makes sense: this toxic person's behavior and way of relating to us seem familiar, and we already know our role and what's expected of us within the relationship.

The good news is that we *can* heal from codependency and rediscover or reinvent ourselves. We can feel self-confident and have healthy self-esteem. We can set personal boundaries and attract healthy, mentally balanced individuals into our lives. We can move forward to have a full and satisfying life experience.

Whether your mom is a narcissist or not, if you're codependent, it's essential to recover from it because it's a maladaptive way to live. Unresolved codependency has the potential to attract mentally unhealthy people into your life. It advertises your low self-esteem, self-worth, and self-confidence, and it suggests that you may tolerate manipulation, maltreatment, and maybe even abuse. If you're codependent, start working to heal it.

TAKEAWAYS

- Codependency has been defined as "a disease of a lost self," and a result of an individual's prolonged exposure to, and practice of, a set of oppressive rules which prevent the open expression of emotions and problems.

- Codependency exists on a continuum, from mild to severe, just as narcissism does. There are three stages along the continuum.

- To feel emotionally and physically safe, it becomes necessary for the child of a narcissistic mother to be hypervigilant and to control outcomes related to the mother's behavior.

- Codependency eventually affects one's ability to have healthy, mutually satisfying adult relationships.

ACTION FOR HEALING

1. Write a letter to your mother that you will never send her. Tell her how she made you feel while you were growing up. Be specific. Let yourself experience any emotions that arise. Don't explain or defend her behavior. Acknowledge that you were a child and had no control over her behavior. Acknowledge that her actions, thoughts, and mental instability are not your fault; you didn't cause them, you can't control them, and you can't cure them.

In your letter, tell her how you feel about her. Describe how your life and relationships have been affected by your childhood.

2. Ask yourself these questions about your current relationships, and journal about your insights:

   - What am I minimizing?

   - What am I tolerating?

   - What am I denying?

3. Begin finding ways of empowering yourself. Stop waiting for validation from others. What others think or believe about you *does not matter.*

4. Acknowledge what your body, mind, and feelings are telling you. Again, this is a way to validate yourself. What you think and feel matters!

5. How can you practice mindfulness regarding how you spend your time? Are you spending time trying to help and fix others? How can you start putting self-care into practice?

6. Allow others the dignity and space to make and learn from their own mistakes.

Chapter Eighteen
TALKING WITH YOUR NARCISSISTIC MOTHER

"As children, we're not allowed to express feelings like anger, and we're certainly not allowed to talk back or disagree. We often can't show happiness, have fun, or be silly without earning her disapproval."

If you feel apprehensive or awkward at the thought of having a serious talk with your mother, it's a signal that you feel unsafe to some degree. Remember, your intuition is there to protect you. It's important to acknowledge what your intuition suggests without judging or assigning any kind of value, such as "bad" or "wrong." Begin to validate yourself by accepting your feelings about talking with your mother and that you have reason to feel the way you do. Recognize that what you sense is valid and honor that. Don't lie to yourself; don't gaslight yourself. This is a turning point for healing. It's time to be real.

As you know by now, if your mother is a narcissist, then it's improbable that you'll be able to have that heart-to-heart conversation with her that you've always longed for. You know the one: where you have a cup of tea or coffee together and just visit peacefully, enjoying each other's company. In your fantasy, you feel lighthearted, and being with her feels easy. You laugh, and you feel safe and comfortable. In your imaginary visit, your mother doesn't judge you, criticize, or make barbed comments, and you don't have to justify and defend your every thought, feeling, or choice. In your fantasy, your mother accepts and supports you, she hears you, she sees you, and you feel as though you matter a great deal to her. You feel secure in knowing she's got your back.

Those of us with narcissistic mothers have those kinds of fantasies. In recovery, we learn to accept that she's simply not capable of this kind of emotional connection, and we begin to let that idea go. In healing, we come to realize that there are and always will be others who want an emotional connection with us, and we nurture those relationships. Some of us may even be fortunate enough to find a mother figure who meets our needs.

No, you won't have that heart-to-heart connection with her, but you *can* learn how to interact without getting hurt or frustrated. You can learn how to protect yourself and minimize the severity of the usual painful exchanges.

Narcissists live by their emotions, and their emotional state dictates how they respond. There is no scientific consensus for a definition of emotion. In this book, emotion is defined as a feeling which has a meaning attached to it. So, a feeling + a chosen meaning = an emotion.

As we know, emotions are not data, and they're not factual. Emotions are chemically driven and are affected by a myriad of variables like environmental stimuli, physical health, age, worldview, self-talk, sleep quality and quantity, stress level, personal experience, food choices, beliefs, memories, thoughts, and much more. Narcissists may understand this, but they can't relate to it.

For example, can the weather cause you to feel an emotion? If you're inside today, cozy and warm, and it begins to storm, do you feel any emotion about it? If you're getting married today and it begins to downpour, you'll likely experience feelings about it. You might be disappointed, angry, or sad, among other things. If you're a farmer, anticipating the end of a drought, you'd be ecstatically happy about the deluge. In each example, the meaning given to "rain" is very different, and the resulting emotion will align with that meaning. As they say, "perspective is everything."

Narcissists have a self-centered perspective, and as their emotions change, their reality changes along with it. They view the present moment in whatever way their emotional filters are presenting it to them, and they're usually going to be a victim. Discussions with a narcissistic mother are frustrating. If your mother is a narcissist, conversations seem futile and pointless. You're not heard, much less understood. Your thoughts, feelings, and opinions are invalidated or mocked. You might even be called names or shouted at.

"You won't have a heart-to-heart connection with your mother, but you can learn how to interact with her successfully."

When emotionally healthy adults disagree with each other, they still speak politely to each other. They use logic, intelligence, good judgment, and skillsets like negotiation, and compromise. In conversations with emotionally immature people like narcissists, this isn't possible. A narcissist mother talks *at* you and doesn't hear what you say. She's preoccupied, thinking of her next response and reviewing the list of ways that you've "wronged her." Because she's driven by emotion and the need to feel admired and superior, she contradicts every point you make.

POINTLESS ARGUMENTS AND EMOTIONALLY EXHAUSTING DISCUSSIONS

Narcissistic moms enjoy having pointless arguments. They love it when we keep explaining, keep trying, and keep showing her that we're emotionally invested in our relationship with her. They love that we care about what she thinks of us. These are forms of narcissistic supply for her. Have you ever had a two-hour argument about nothing? They're a form of supply; she's getting rejuvenated while you're being drained.

To minimize the possibility of a time-wasting, emotionally exhausting discussion, particular actions need to be taken before, during, and after talking with your narcissistic mother.

CRAZY-MAKING CONVERSATIONS

From now on, conversations with your mom need to be planned. You'll need to strategize. This sounds ridiculous when you consider you're going through all of this trouble just to have a conversation with your mother. It shouldn't be this difficult, right? You might even feel anger or resentment because of all the extra time and planning it will take to have a civil conversation with her. I get it, and it's OK to feel that way. I did too.

What you're doing here is taking back your power. You're thinking about the different scenarios and the twists and turns the conversation could take, and you're preparing to handle them with grace and dignity.

You're attempting to maximize the possibility of having a drama-free discussion, and that's an honorable thing to do. It's not about your mother; it's about you. You're going to take back your power and run this show. Focus on what you want that to look like and use the tools available. These tools include limiting your expectations, setting personal boundaries, and knowing and controlling your emotional triggers.

You need to be comfortable setting your expectations and boundaries for this conversation. Don't try this until you've done the work regarding expectations and boundaries.

You need to be aware of your emotional triggers and have a plan for what you'll do if you get triggered. The last thing you want to do is lose control of your emotions. Remember—*your emotional outburst is her narcissistic supply*. If you lose control of yourself, that will be a reward for her. Do *not* reward her. The whole idea here is to *deny* her any narcissistic supply so that you can have a drama-free conversation.

At first, you might feel anxious about setting the rules of engagement for your talk. With practice, it becomes more comfortable each time, and you'll want to continue doing it because it works.

Here's a general outline for preparing for a conversation with your narcissistic mother. I developed this strategy and tweaked it over the years, and I've had great success with it:

- Set the date. Choose a day and time when you're likely to feel confident and centered. The more you practice mindfulness, becoming aware of your moods, triggers, cycles, etc. the more self-aware you'll become.

- Set start and end times for the conversation. Be prepared to stick to the time frame.

- Limit the length of contact and keep it brief. Estimate how much time this conversation would typically take with someone other than your mom and aim for that amount.

- Set ground rules (boundaries) around how you'd like the conversation to flow.

- Notify your mother (or not). If her schedule fluctuates, or you're meeting at a designated spot, you'll need her cooperation to schedule a get-together. If you interact with her regularly, you won't need to set a formal date, unless you feel strongly that you should. (Personally, I wouldn't give any indication that something different or unexpected is about to happen.)

- Be ready to end the conversation early. It's OK if that happens.

- Every interaction with a narcissist has a cost. Know and accept what that cost will probably be for you.

Before you meet:

- Strategize: know what you want to talk about and the points you want to make. Have your facts ready.

- Examine and understand your expectations for this discussion and revise them where necessary. I've heard expectations defined as "premeditated resentments." Try not to have expectations. If you don't expect a particular outcome, you can't be disappointed.

- Set personal boundaries regarding the behaviors you will and will not accept from your mother. Have a plan for how you'll respond if she exhibits unacceptable behaviors.

- Know what activates your emotional triggers. Have a planned response for when your mother starts pushing those buttons, so you're not caught off guard and succumb to the attack.

- Practice the conversation alone or with a trusted family member or friend, but practice!

The day of:

- Understand your topic of conversation and why you chose it. Review your expectations and your boundaries again.

- Review your triggers and what you'll do if you get triggered.

- Take a deep breath, meditate, or do whatever makes you feel grounded.

- Visualize the conversation going the way you want it to. Envision your personal power as an interior ball of energy. Imagine a control panel to vary the level of power and crank it up until it's radiating brightly, enveloping you. Keep this image with you throughout your meeting.

Before your conversation:

- Go over the ground rules (boundaries) with her. Do this calmly, respectfully, and firmly whether it's the first time or the hundredth. Your mother needs to be aware of the requirements necessary for the conversation to continue. She needs to know that if she doesn't adhere to them, the discussion will end immediately when the boundary is broken. She doesn't need to agree with this. This is *your* boundary, and it's for you, not her. For example, you can say something like: "I know in the past when we've disagreed, it ended badly. I don't want that to happen again. It's important to me that we listen to and hear each other, and respect each other's feelings, so if we can't maintain a calm and respectful tone, I will leave."

   Now, this is really important: if you say you will leave when the boundary is broken, then you absolutely have to leave. Don't argue back. Don't defend yourself. Don't explain. When that boundary of calm and respect has been broken, you just get up and go. There is no explanation necessary because you already *gave it* before the conversation started.

It's important to honor your boundaries; otherwise, you're teaching your mother that you're "all talk but no action." It hurts the first time you enforce a boundary. It hurts the next time too. But here' my point: if you're consistent, your mother will learn that she can't treat you poorly anymore. Whether she likes it or not, she'll learn that she must honor your boundaries *if* she wants to have any interaction with you at all.

Training your mother to behave differently with you takes time and repetition. There's nothing more frustrating to her than pushing your buttons and getting no response, no *supply* from you. It's not going to happen on the first attempt. To make her understand that you're serious, you'll need to enforce your boundaries repeatedly. Keep in mind that she's not becoming empathetic, more understanding, or more emotionally attached to you. Those are complex changes that she's not capable of. What's actually happening is much more straightforward. She's learning that her source of supply goes away when she does x, y, or z.

During the conversation:

- Be direct. Speak assertively.

- Make factual statements. Do not explain your feelings or your choices. Explaining yourself only serves to feed your mother's ego and give her more attention and supply.

- Do not defend or justify. *Do not provide any supply.*

- Maintain your boundaries.

- Stay in your power. Remember, you will act with dignity and grace in your personal power. *It does not matter how she chooses to act.*

Don't forget; your mother has a right to her own thoughts and perceptions of you. This isn't about trying to get her to see you or accept you. This is about saying what you want to tell her.

There will be times that you'll need to appear indifferent to her words or actions, to deny her any emotional supply. A powerful technique for doing this is called "Gray Rock," a term coined in 2012 by Skylar, a blogger who wrote the article, "The Gray Rock Method of Dealing with Psychopaths" (2018).

Gray Rock is a technique that causes emotionally unbalanced people to lose interest in you. The method completely removes any emotional charge or drama from your interaction with them. When you use Gray Rock, it removes all narcissistic supply.

To use the Gray Rock method:

- Appear calm, even if you're not.

- Maintain eye contact. Do not look down or away.

- Use the following examples when applicable:

  o   I'm sorry you feel that way.

  o   I can accept your distorted view of me.

  o   I welcome your opinion, but I feel good about my choice.

  o   I have no right to try to control how you see me.

  o   I accept how you see me.

- I accept how you feel.

- You're entitled to your reality.

- Your anger is not my responsibility.

- Your anger is not my problem.

- It's possible. I guess it could be true.

- I'd like to continue this discussion, but it seems that we don't share the same perspective. Maybe when you're calm, we can resume this conversation in a mutually respectful way. (This is an example of enforcing a boundary.)

A tool that I use in my own recovery is responding calmly with something like, "I understand you feel that way," and then I *shut up*.

This tool (shutting up/staying quiet/not responding) works because it removes the emotional response that I really want to give my mother. It denies her any supply. If Mom pushes my buttons in an attempt to trigger me, I will not answer, I do not take the bait, my mouth remains shut. I do this consistently and repeatedly because it indicates that I'm OK with whatever response she provides and that I will *not* react to it. Not engaging, not defending, not arguing back takes mindfulness and practice, but it's worth the time and effort. It's part of "loving detachment" and maintaining your boundaries.

Having a conversation with a narcissistic mother feels like a game of emotional tug-of-war. But when you drop your end of the rope, the game stops. It can't continue unless you pick up your end and start pulling again. So, no more games. You don't have to explain that you're no longer playing or why. Your actions speak loud and clear: when you drop the rope, you're demonstrating that she no longer has control over you.

If you haven't tried this, I can tell you from experience that it's very empowering.

After the conversation:

Take some quiet time alone to review how it went and how you feel. Journal about the conversation's pros and cons. Talk about how it went well and how it didn't. Write about what you'll need to do differently the next time you get together. Write it out, review it, and use it the next time you spend time with your mother. Doing these will build the consistency that it takes. Each time you interact, you'll make those little tweaks and changes, and eventually, you'll have a solid way of conversing with your mom that isn't extremely painful or frustrating to you.

Takeaways

- You can talk with your narcissistic mother without getting hurt or frustrated, or minimize the severity of those.

- Narcissists have a self-centered perspective. As their emotions change, their reality changes along with it. They view the present moment in whatever way their emotional filters are presenting it.

- Narcissistic moms enjoy having pointless arguments. It's entertaining for them and a source of narcissistic supply. She gets rejuvenated while you become drained.

- To minimize the possibility of a time-wasting, emotionally exhausting discussion, particular actions need to be taken before, during, and after talking with your narcissistic mother.

Action for Healing

1. Work on self-acceptance. Start to adopt new attitudes about yourself now, so they become part of your healthier thought and behavior pattern. Remember, it's about progress, not perfection.

2. Begin to experiment with assertively expressing your needs and using the statements from the Gray Rock technique.

3. You're getting ready to let go of your existence as a passive target and become the active creator of your life. Start to experiment with setting healthy boundaries and limits.

Chapter Nineteen
ADDRESSING PTSD and C-PTSD

"PTSD is a whole-body tragedy, an integral human event of enormous proportions with massive repercussions."

—Susan Pease Banitt

THE DIFFERENCE BETWEEN PTSD AND C-PTSD

Post-traumatic stress disorder (PTSD) is usually related to a single traumatic event. Complex post-traumatic stress disorder (C-PTSD) results from a series of trauma-causing events, or one prolonged event. With C-PTSD, the repeated exposure to trauma causes additional symptoms not experienced by those who have PTSD.

C-PTSD can be the result of ongoing narcissistic trauma and abuse. Who we are at our core, our very being, is continually threatened when we're in a narcissistic relationship.

Children who experience neglect or ongoing traumatic abuse are at risk of developing C-PTSD, as well as depression, self-harming behaviors, and anxiety. They're also at risk for conduct, attachment, eating, and substance use disorders. As we've learned, when these children become adults, they'll be at risk for revictimization. They'll also have a higher risk of developing physical illnesses like diabetes, heart disease, and immunological disorders. Research shows that women who've endured childhood abuse-related PTSD may also have altered brain structures. Their cognitive functioning may be impaired as compared with women who were abused but not diagnosed with PTSD, or women with no history of abuse.

Common symptoms of C-PTSD are flashbacks, panic attacks, nightmares, excessive startle reaction, and routinely thinking about the traumatic event

—McCllelland and Gilyard 2008

Abuse-related stress and trauma are associated with a reduced ability to focus and categorize information. When the attention and memory encoding activities of the amygdala and hippocampus cease due to real or perceived threats, verbal language ability may also be harmed (Ford 2017).

Complex Post Traumatic Stress Disorder (C-PTSD), is called a disorder of "extreme stress not otherwise specified" in the DSM-5 and is a relatively new term. Some mental health practitioners would like C-PTSD to have its own diagnostic criteria, separate from those of PTSD. This change may actually be forthcoming. A possible indicator is that PTSD was removed from the "anxiety disorders" category and added to a brand new section called "trauma and stress-related disorders" in the DSM-5 (Gattuso 2018).

PTSD symptoms are stress-related coping mechanisms called "triggers," which are associated with hypervigilance (Lanius et al. 2010). PTSD symptoms include but aren't limited to:

- angry outbursts

- self-destructive behavior

- flashbacks of the event

- nightmares

- disturbing memories

- avoiding similar situations or people

- difficulty concentrating

- feeling "jumpy" or startling easily

- depression

- emotional numbness

PTSD can also include bodily symptoms like nausea, headaches, dizziness, chest pains, stomach aches, and sudden rapid heartbeat.

We've established that narcissistic mothers intentionally look for and exploit their children's weaknesses, which may cause them to feel confused, anxious, and unsafe. Living in such a destructive environment is like trying to survive in a war zone. If we're in this situation, we exist in a state of continued heightened stress. We never know when the next attack will come or in what form, but based on previous experience, we know it's coming. When we live in an unpredictable environment, where we're invalidated, threatened, bullied, intimidated, ignored, shamed, blamed, lied to, betrayed, or physically harmed, as we've seen, we go into fight-or-flight survival mode. This, combined with an active fear of abandonment, contributes to the development of C-PTSD.

C-PTSD results from a series of traumatic occurrences or a single prolonged traumatic event. Our brains store the distressing information, to alert us to possible threats in the future. Those who have C-PTSD learn how to avoid or repress painful memories by emotionally numbing them: they actively avoid, deny, disconnect from, and reject the traumatic memories (Phillips 2015). The trauma remains unaddressed.

People who have C-PTSD experience the PTSD symptoms listed above, along with additional symptoms such as:

- feelings of shame or guilt

- feelings of responsibility for the abuse

- difficulty controlling emotions

- loss of attention and focus (dissociation)

- isolation from friends and family

- relationship difficulties

- destructive or risky behavior, such as alcohol or drug abuse

- suicidal thoughts

- unnecessary worrying

- adrenal burnout

- chronic inflammatory disorders

- mental exhaustion

- various forms of anxiety

- weight loss or weight gain

- self-gaslighting

Those of us who've experienced maternal narcissism and the resulting C-PTSD symptoms do so because our minds are attempting to ensure our safety. Remember, traumatic experiences are not stored linearly as stories but as fragments of sensory input: smells, sights, sounds, touches, tastes.

With C-PTSD, these stored fragments become triggers, the highly sensitive, reactive emotions that become activated by our environment or someone's behavior or words. Triggers alert us to recurring dangers or threats. When we become triggered, we automatically react without any thought, often feeling like we're losing control. When we become triggered because of C-PTSD, it becomes challenging to navigate our daily lives and relationships.

If we're triggered, we may quietly emotionally withdraw, or we may react intensely and aggressively. Either way, it's because we're defending ourselves against a perceived threat, whether it's a real threat or just feels like one.

Our emotional triggers are wounds that still need to heal. For example, your friend makes a casual remark, and for some reason, you suddenly and without warning, hear yourself snap back with a cutting and intentionally hurtful remark. You don't know what came over you. You weren't in a bad mood or feeling angry, but as the comment was made, you immediately reacted swiftly, instinctively, and defensively to protect yourself. You intuitively understand that you wounded and confused your friend, but you don't know why you did it. Later, after you've taken the time to reflect on and process the event, you realize that at the moment you heard the comment, you instantly felt distraught, under attack, defensive, angry, confused, or full of self-doubt. It was as if a switch had been flipped.

In hindsight, you also recognize that the remark was not said to hurt you intentionally, and yet you deliberately reacted viciously, with a desire to inflict pain. You decide to apologize to your friend because now you understand that the remark activated one of your triggers, and *your* triggers are *your responsibility.*

Get to know your triggers. We can never know all of them because we're usually not aware of them until they happen. Triggers are created with consistency and repetition. We develop new ones throughout life because we're continually partaking in new life experiences. Once you have an idea of what some of your triggers are, though, you can form appropriate responses to have ready for the next time. Sometimes just having an awareness that you've been triggered is enough to keep a reaction in check. You can eliminate your triggers by determining that they're no longer valid. For example, get rid of the unrealistic expectations and values that trigger you. Cut yourself some slack. You are not perfect. Your life is not perfect. Let go of expectations of perfection. There is no such thing as perfection. Like everyone else, you're an imperfect being who doesn't know everything and never will, but you're learning and growing every day. Isn't that enough?

CHILDHOOD DEVELOPMENT AND ATTACHMENT STYLES

Erik H. Erikson (1902–1994) was a German-American developmental psychologist known for an eight-stage theory of human social development. He hypothesized that in each stage, children confront new challenges and (hopefully) learn to master them. Each step depends on successfully completing the previous ones. When a child experiences trauma in any of these phases, it can mean that the phase will not be completed successfully.

The phases that aren't successfully completed will often reappear as future adult issues.

Erikson's eight stages include an age range and the challenges that must be met within that timeframe:

- Age 0–1: Trust vs. Mistrust

- Age 2–3: Autonomy vs. Shame and Doubt

- Age 3–6: Initiative vs. Guilt

- Age 7–12: Industry vs. Inferiority

- Age 12–18: Identity vs. Role Confusion

- Age 20–45: Intimacy vs. Isolation

- Age 30–65: Generativity vs. Stagnation

- Age 50+: Ego Integrity vs. Despair

It's beyond the scope of this book to delve into each phase and the possible outcomes. If you're curious, I hope you'll take a more in-depth look into Erikson's stages of development.

Since Erikson, there's been a lot of research in the field of early childhood development, regarding trauma and abuse. The effects of a traumatic childhood on future adult behavior and relationships have been well documented. Two contemporary psychologists, John Bowlby and Mary Ainsworth have contributed much to our current understanding of this connection. Their research reveals how unmet childhood emotional needs can impact their future mental health and relationships.

John Bowlby (1907–1990) was a British psychologist and psychoanalyst known for his "childhood attachments" theory. He performed extensive research on the concept of attachment and described it as a "lasting psychological connectedness between human beings" (Bowlby 1969).

Bowlby believed that attachment behavior is a survival mechanism and a result of evolution. He theorized that childhood experiences directly influence adult development and behavior, and concluded that individual attachment styles are established in early childhood wholly through infant/caregiver relationships.

His research and that of psychologist Mary Ainsworth contribute to the current body of work known as "attachment theory."

According to Bowlby, the attachment phase takes place in the first three years of life. His research indicates that to develop a healthy sense of self, including a foundation for forming healthy adult relationships, we must feel safe in our key caregiver relationships. So, if a child experiences C-PTSD, it could be from an early caregiver relationship that was scary, chaotic, threatening, or absent. These kinds of experiences may negatively impact the child's ability to form secure attachments in the future.

Survivors of complex childhood trauma often have difficulty forming attachments to other people. This struggle creates a self-perpetuating cycle: an unfulfilled desire for connection leads to loneliness and isolation, which can lead to depression, risky, and self-destructive behaviors, which can lead to loneliness and isolation. It makes sense that the treatment process for C-PTSD includes learning how to strengthen one's ability to feel attached while also feeling safe, secure, and loved. It is "an extremely difficult process" but not impossible to achieve (Franco 2018).

In 1970, Dr. Ainsworth expanded on Bowlby's work in her paper "Attachment, Exploration, and Separation: Illustrated by The Behavior of One-Year-Olds in a Strange Situation." In her research, she discovered three major attachment styles: secure, ambivalent-insecure, and avoidant-insecure attachment (Ainsworth and Bell 1970). They were expanding on that research in 1986 when Drs. Mary Main and Judith

Solomon added a fourth attachment style called "disorganized-insecure attachment" (Main and Solomon 1986). Additional research supports their conclusions and the idea that early attachment styles can predict future behavior.

THE FOUR ATTACHMENT STYLES

The following is a description of the four attachment styles as per Drs. Ainsworth, Main, and Solomon:

A secure attachment style forms when a primary caregiver is mainly predictable, reliable, and trustworthy. If a parent or caregiver is a source of comfort, the child feels relaxed as they discover, learn, and play in their environment. When they reach adulthood, they're able to develop meaningful connections with others and confidently deal with the inevitable relationship disagreements.

An ambivalent-insecure attachment style forms when a primary caregiver is unreliable, erratic, or unpredictable. There are times the child feels cared for, interspersed with times of being shouted at or rejected (intermittent conditioning). This kind of relationship leaves the child feeling indecisive, hesitant, or doubtful. When they reach adulthood, they may feel a sense of dependency and fear of abandonment in their close relationships.

An avoidant-insecure attachment style forms when a primary caregiver is disengaged, distant, and unavailable. The child's needs go unmet or are ignored, and they learn to take care of themselves, becoming self-reliant. When they reach adulthood, they may have a dismissive attitude toward others' emotional needs or lack the ability to experience emotional intimacy.

A disorganized-attachment style forms when a primary caregiver is chaotic and abusive. The caregiver is not a source of love and nurturing, but of fear and concern. Kids will still attach to an aggressive, cruel, or abusive parent because we're all born with a need for closeness. But we also have a strong need to avoid danger. A child in this position will likely develop feelings of helplessness and hopelessness because they're caught in the middle; they need and desire attachment and also need to escape danger. When they reach adulthood, they will likely alternate between feeling fear and anger or defeat and depression.

We learn how to develop healthy, supportive relationships by interacting with our primary caretakers and family members. Kids who've been neglected, mistreated, or abused by a caretaker find it challenging to form a healthy attachment to them. If our caretaker was emotionally unstable, neglectful, or abusive, we might have learned that we can't trust or depend on others to meet our needs. Studies indicate that children are more susceptible to stress and its related illnesses when they're unable to create a healthy attachment to their caretaker. They may have difficulty interacting with authority figures like teachers and other adults. They struggle with managing and expressing their emotions, and they may react inappropriately or even aggressively in specific settings. Later in life, they may have difficulty sustaining romantic relationships and friendships.

It's common to repeat the first relational patterns and attachment styles we learned as children (Schwartz 2019). Most of us have a combination style of attachment because we often have more than one parent or caretaker. Each of them treats us differently, and so we develop a combination of the four attachment styles.

Takeaways

- PTSD symptoms are stress-related coping mechanisms called triggers.

- Triggers are stored memory fragments of traumatic events, and they alert us to recurring danger or threats. Our triggers signify wounds that still need to heal.

- C-PTSD results from a series of traumatic occurrences or a single prolonged traumatic event. People who have C-PTSD experience the symptoms of PTSD, but also suffer additional symptoms.

- The effects that traumatic childhoods have on adult behavior and relationships have been well documented.

- It's common to repeat the first relational patterns and attachment styles we learned as children.

Action for Healing

1. Continue taking steps to identify your triggers:

    - Deepen your practice of mindfulness to become aware of each trigger and when or where it appears.

    - Give some thought to how each trigger may have formed and how it protected you.

    - Think of ways to respond to each trigger rather than letting it take over your emotional response.

2. Look into a type of therapy called "inner child" work:

   - In your journal, list the negative messages you heard as a child.

   - Think about whether they're accurate now and whether they were ever true. Write about your insights.

3. Karyl McBride, Ph.D. states that "specialized recovery involves cleaning up trauma first and accepting that your parent is not going to change. The change will be within you" (McBride, 2013). Actively recovering from trauma includes three essential pieces. Have you begun doing them?

   - Understanding the problem's background, history, and diagnosis

   - Dealing with feelings associated with that background and history

   - Reframing the past to change your current world-perspective.

PART III
MAKE LEMONADE

Chapter Twenty
SETTING PERSONAL BOUNDARIES

"Love yourself enough to set boundaries. Your time and energy are precious. You get to choose how you use it. You teach people how to treat you by deciding what you will and won't accept."

—Anna Taylor

Personally, I believe that setting personal boundaries is the first step in healing from codependency. When we don't have limits, we can be taken advantage of. If we lack boundaries, we may deny our thoughts or feelings just to gain someone's approval or acceptance. These are self-limiting behaviors and don't work for our betterment.

Boundaries protect us from someone else's behavior or from engaging in activities that we'd rather not. Setting healthy boundaries is a form of self-care because, in doing so, we get to determine what's acceptable to us and what's not. They help us set limits that protect and empower us. Personal boundaries pertain to "you" rather than others. For example, my boundaries are for and about me, nobody else. They're about "what I need" to maintain my safety, emotional stability, and mental health, and they're under *my* control.

Your boundaries are based on *your* needs and are about maintaining your sense of safety, emotional stability, and mental health. Boundaries are not something you negotiate. *You* get to determine what's acceptable to you and what's not.

It takes courage to decide, "No, I won't put up with, or do that, anymore." It means we're taking the first step to end the people-pleasing, and maybe for the first time, we're willing to accept the many ways (good and bad) that people might respond to this.

Setting boundaries can feel scary because sometimes the stakes are high. Others, who've counted on your lack of limits, probably won't like you focusing on your life instead of them. They may not like this "new you." They may be angry or resentful or criticize, judge, or shame you. That's OK. They're entitled to have their own thoughts and feelings about you. However, remember, their views and opinions are "their stuff," not your stuff, and are none of your business. Not your circus, not your clowns.

YES AND NO

Saying "no" is a boundary and a choice. Saying "I won't do that" or "I will no longer tolerate _____" is a way to honor yourself and your feelings.

When we're codependent, we often say yes when we want to say no, or vice versa, and that can make us feel resentful, used, and angry. You lose your authenticity when you don't say what you mean and mean what you say. Why do we do this? I think it's because we're afraid of the other person's possible reaction or having to justify or explain ourselves. But really, an explanation isn't required.

"No" is a complete sentence. It's an affirmation of our integrity and authenticity.

In order to heal codependency, it's essential to start saying what you mean and meaning what you say. I've heard it said that our yes is stronger and more meaningful if we say no now and then. When you say no, you can do it with love and compassion; it doesn't have to be mean.

It's far more empowering to use an "assertive no" rather than a "submissive yes." Think about that. You're the one in control of where to draw the line and how to state where you stand. It's empowering to establish parameters around the kinds of conduct you will and will not accept from others.

How to Set Boundaries with Your Mother

Boundaries are not intended to be a way of controlling your mother, and they're not meant to change her behavior. They're a way to set personal limits for ourselves. They're not emotional; they're factual. They're not a threat issued to control her, but they are your "line in the sand."

Setting boundaries with your mother means that you've thought about her style of interacting with and relating to you, and you've determined what's acceptable to you and what's not.

Your healthy boundary gives your mother the ability to make choices, *including* breaking the boundary and experiencing the consequences.

Setting a boundary requires three steps:

1. Acknowledging that you have a specific physical or emotional unmet need to feel happy, safe, healthy, loved, understood, etc. For example, you need to feel safe.

2. Recognize her behavior that directly conflicts with meeting this need. For example, your mother shouts at you, and you feel threatened and unsafe when she does this.

3. Establish consequences for unacceptable behavior. When that line is crossed, you need to know what to do ahead of time and be prepared to do it. Using the example above, the consequences for shouting at you are that you physically leave as soon as she raises her voice.

A consequence is an action *you* take to protect *yourself*, to take *you* out of the situation. You need to be aware that by following through with the consequence, you'll be letting the scene play out without you. By setting a boundary, it means you'll no longer engage with the problematic behavior. Instead, you lay down your end of the tug-of-war rope, and do something else. What the other person decides to do next is up to them.

In this scenario, you respect your need to feel safe, and you don't feel safe when your mother shouts at you. Your boundary is: "I will no longer tolerate her shouting at me." The consequence is: "I will leave at the first sign of shouting." What your mother does next is irrelevant. Your need to feel safe and your boundary for meeting that need is your priority. Your boundary is for you, and what your mother chooses next is not your responsibility.

"Boundaries work both ways: you will no longer violate others' boundaries by rescuing, or trying to fix them or their circumstances."

We must accept that we have no control over what happens after we remove ourselves from a situation. AND we must recognize that no matter what happens, we won't step back in and try to take control.

This is the terrifying part because, *of course*, what happens next could affect you. This fear can make us want to give up the idea of setting boundaries and just remain codependent.

As an adult, you do not need your mother's permission, validation, or recognition to set boundaries for yourself. You do not need to submit proof that you are being hurt in your relationship with her.

A healthy boundary should give your mother some choices. If there is only one option open to her, then it's not a healthy boundary. It's more of a threat or ultimatum.

- State your need (For example, "I need to feel safe when I talk with my mom.")

- State the behavior that conflicts with your need. (For example, "I don't feel safe when she calls me hurtful names.")

- State the consequence for the behavior. (For example, "I'll end the call if she starts name-calling.")

Ask yourself:

- Does the boundary take care of me?

- Am I trying to control my mother's behavior, or am I trying to take care of myself? Is my "boundary" a type of threat or ultimatum? If so, you'll need to re-work it.

Start with just one boundary and see how it goes. It takes practice to set them, especially if we didn't learn how when we were kids or if we've never seen healthy boundaries in action. Sometimes the boundaries or their consequences will need to be tweaked or adjusted, so they work better. That's absolutely OK! Just make sure that whatever your consequence is, you will absolutely carry it out. If we back down or don't enforce our own boundaries, we can end up feeling defeated, resentful, or weak. When we don't enforce our own boundaries, we're sending the message that we're not serious about it.

If you're not able to carry out the consequence, then you need a different consequence.

Takeaways

- Setting healthy personal boundaries is the first step in healing from codependency. It is a form of self-care; boundaries protect and empower us.

- A healthy boundary gives your mother the ability to make choices, including breaking the boundary and experiencing the consequences.

- When we're healing from codependency, it's essential to start saying what we mean and meaning what we say.

- Setting boundaries is a way of affirming your authentic self and demonstrating integrity.

- Setting a boundary requires three steps.

- You do not need your mother's permission, validation, or recognition to set boundaries for yourself.

Action for Healing

1. Identify a need that is not being met. (For example, you need to feel emotionally and physically safe around your mother.)

2. Which of your mother's behaviors keep this need unmet? (For example, she loses her temper and throws objects.)

3. Set a consequence around this behavior. (For example, you will leave her house and go home.)

Example of a healthy boundary:

What you need: "I need to feel safe when I'm around my mother."

Her behavior: outbursts and rages.

Her consequence for engaging in the behavior: If she starts to lose her temper, I will leave and go to the park to calm down.

Chapter Twenty-one
IDENTIFYING DANGEROUS PEOPLE

"Experience is the hardest kind of teacher. It gives you the test first and the lesson afterward."

—Vernon Law

When it comes to healing, we've seen the importance of identifying codependent thoughts and behaviors and replacing them. We've learned the importance of creating personal boundaries around behavior that we're no longer willing to tolerate, and we're beginning to see the connection between gaslighting, codependency, trauma bonds, C-PTSD, attachment styles, and our future health and relationships. Identifying toxic people and unhealthy relationships is another essential step in healing from narcissistic abuse.

RECOGNIZING TOXIC PEOPLE

If you were affected by, and begin recovering from the effects of gaslighting, codependency, or C-PTSD, your self-care will become more important to you. It's imperative to learn how to recognize toxic or dangerous individuals and limit your exposure to them, as part of taking care of yourself.

The WEB Method, a "quick and easy way to identify potentially dangerous people," was developed by a licensed social worker, Bill Eddy. According to Eddy, there are three things to examine if you think there's a chance an individual may be narcissistic, toxic, or unsafe. The method requires you to pay attention to words the individual speaks, to your emotions, and to *their* behavior (Eddy 2018).

"Paying attention to their words" means you should:

- Notice if they use either extremely positive or extremely negative words to describe you or others. This indicates black and white thinking, a trait of narcissists, and those who have a borderline personality disorder.

- Monitor for words that indicate a lack of emotional empathy or lack of interest in others. Again, narcissistic traits, as well as those of sociopaths and psychopaths.

- Spot words that indicate that they see themselves as a victim or that they think they've been duped, targeted, or wounded. These are traits of narcissists as well as of individuals who blame, make excuses, shirk responsibility, harbor resentment, and practice negative self-talk. You've made a lot of progress and come too far to let yourself get involved with a "poor me.".

PAY ATTENTION

Notice if they virtue signal. Virtue signaling is the not-so-humble declaring of one's morals and values. "I'm generous," "I'm extremely open-minded," "I'm a good person." These could be examples of "words not matching actions." When someone wants others to believe what they say about themselves, rather than how they act, it's a type of gaslighting. Most of us don't need to talk about or convince others of our good qualities. When a person possesses admirable character and integrity, they don't need to announce or advertise it. They simply live it, and people notice.

"Paying attention to your emotions" means checking in with your feelings:

- How do you feel when you're around the person? Confused? Drained? Hurt? Defeated? Misunderstood? Stupid? Inadequate? Bullied? Mocked? Belittled? Humiliated?

- Does it feel "too good to be true?" Charm is considered to be a warning sign. People who intensely or endlessly flatter, praise, or compliment are often being manipulative. Charm may indicate that they're a deceptive or controlling person.

- Do you feel like you can't catch your breath or you can't think? Narcissists often overwhelm others with their posturing and self-directed focus. They dominate conversations, don't allow differences of opinion, and keep the focus on themselves. Conversations often feel like debates, and it's usually hard to change the subject or disengage. When you're in discussion with a narcissist, you'll feel unheard, misunderstood, dismissed, or be mocked or ridiculed if you challenge or disagree with them.

"Paying attention to their behavior" means you need to:

- Focus on their actions. Narcissists are defensive and will attack those who criticize or challenge them. Look at how they treat people. Notice if they embarrass you or cause you to want to apologize for their behavior.

- Notice their dismissal, disregard, or indifference of yourself or others. Do they interrupt you? Talk over you? Scorn or minimize your point of view? Do they send the message that what they say or do is more important than anything or anybody else? These indicate an ego-centered world view.

- Notice if they blame others for their own mistakes or poor choices. Narcissists and poor-me's are famous for being big blamers.

- Notice if they encourage others to admire them. Do they seek attention, compliments, praise, and admiration? These are all forms of narcissistic supply.

By now, it's plain to see that the process of healing is a complex undertaking. It requires commitment, patience, and time. I genuinely believe it is not a journey to be taken alone because it's easy to get stuck along the way. Professional mental health facilitators and support groups are invaluable to keep you moving in the direction of recovery.

Takeaways

- There is a quick and easy proactive way called the WEB method, to identify toxic, narcissistic, or dangerous individuals.

- The WEB method requires paying close attention to an individual's words, your emotions, and their behavior. Doing this can provide information as to whether the person is potentially dangerous.

Action for Healing

1. Ongoing exercise: Identify people, places, and things that are healthy and useful to your life today, and those that are not.

2. Use the WEB method with new people you meet, as well as those you've known for a while—journal about your insights, thoughts, and feelings.

3. Begin minimizing or breaking contact with people whom the WEB method reveals to be potentially unsafe.

Chapter Twenty-two
YOU GOTTA FEEL IT TO HEAL IT

"I'm here. I'm alive. I'm grateful. I'm ready."

CREATING YOUR HEALING SPACE

Your healing process needs to be a judgment-free zone. You've had unique childhood experiences, and the length of time it takes to recover can't be predetermined. When we start walking the recovery path, we have no idea what we'll discover along the way, and we'll need to acknowledge and heal each of those things. We can't put a time-frame on the progression of events that will take place, set a calendar-goal around them, or compare our progress to anyone else's. Your healing journey is yours alone. This self-focused and insightful time will become a forever part of your life experience, and of you. Welcome whatever you discover, let yourself feel thankful for this opportunity and grateful for the process. Be kind to yourself as you learn and grow.

You've got this. ☺

The process of healing can hurt a lot of the time, but with each breakthrough, I think you should recognize and celebrate; acknowledge that you really *are* making progress. You're doing this productive and healthy thing for yourself because you want to put the past behind you and move forward. You want to develop a healthy mindset and intact boundaries. When you've done your healing work, you'll recognize narcissists and toxic people for what they are, and you'll know how to deal with them when they appear in your life.

If you grew up with a narcissistic mother, you've been hurt, and you've probably witnessed events and experienced distress in ways most people will never know or understand. Sometimes we're so accustomed to being mistreated that we start to think of ourselves as victims. "Victim" might become our identity and how we experience ourselves. When we expect to be victimized, we're seldom surprised when we are. Some of us come to enjoy the sympathy or attention that being a victim can bring.

But living in a state of victimhood is damaging. Thinking of or perceiving ourselves in this way keeps us focused *on our limitations*. This type of cognitive distortion can lead us to give up our personal power and cause us to think, perceive, and behave like dependent children.

Living in a healthy, recovered state means we reclaim our power, set healthy boundaries for ourselves, and make choices based on what *we* need, want, and is good for *us*.

When you're *not* healed, and you openly disclose your thoughts, feelings, beliefs, and ideas to others, you're in a place of vulnerability. You're open to being triggered or re-traumatized if you open up to people who're currently in narcissistic relationships themselves, or who haven't recovered from the effects of their own trauma or abuse. You may unintentionally trigger them, and they may respond hurtfully or inappropriately. They may lash out, invalidate or judge you. Be careful when choosing to share the very private and personal aspects of your childhood. Try to ascertain whether the person you choose to talk with is emotionally stable and can maintain healthy boundaries.

As you recover from the effects of your childhood trauma, you'll become discerning about who you can trust with your openness. You'll discover that emotionally healthy people are able to hear you and interact respectfully with you, and unhealthy people are not. And as you heal, you'll become OK with people detaching from you. You'll understand and be comfortable knowing that you can't control how others perceive you, while at the same time, you'll understand that you don't *need* anyone's validation.

As you heal, what others think or feel about you becomes irrelevant. This is freedom. This is recovery.

So, the big question is: are you ready to heal? Are you ready to take back your personal power? Are you ready for a huge perspective shift? How do you know?

What do you think will change about your personality, or how you think and perceive, after you've gone through the healing process? What might change about your personal goals, your work, and your relationships, if you actually *heal* your childhood wounds?

Imagine what your life might look like after your recovery work. Certain things really will be different. What do you want them to be? *How* might they be different? Besides yourself, who else will be affected by these changes? How? Are you ready to get started?

What Healing Is and Is Not

Healing isn't just the "after" that follows the "before." Healing requires effort and courage.

Healing isn't the deletion of pain or the memories. Healing doesn't erase what happened. It certainly doesn't wipe away the memories, or your feelings and thoughts about your mother or childhood experiences. Healing isn't about forgetting.

Healing is about reframing your painful and traumatic experiences so that they add new depth and meaning to your personal story. If you were able to erase those experiences, you'd also erase a huge opportunity for personal growth and development.

> *"Healing is about reframing your painful and traumatic experiences so that they add new depth and meaning to your personal story."*

In the process of healing, we take the painful memories and experiences and create a whole new perspective and understanding around them.

When we walk through the pain and come out on the other side, we bear the scar of that journey. It'll be a permanent reminder of what we've survived, and it will always be part of us. But the scar won't define us. It'll simply be a small part of our personal story.

Without that story or that experience, we wouldn't be who we are today.

Recuperating from abuse requires us to be willing to become new and better versions of ourselves. Being able to forgive our mothers is an important part of this process, but so is cultivating the ability to forgive ourselves. We need to forgive ourselves because we might have unknowingly, or knowingly, hurt others as a result of our unhealed or unacknowledged childhood wounds.

Healing gives us back the capacity to trust ourselves. As we recover, we'll begin to trust our judgment and make sound decisions. We'll begin to trust others too.

When we avoid the healing process, our emotional triggers often become more sensitive. We're easily triggered, and we end up putting even more emotional energy into self-avoidance to evade the triggers. It becomes a cycle of hiding from and denying pain any time pain is felt. Eventually, we might turn to substances or particular activities to avoid the pain; alcohol, drugs, food, sex, shopping, gambling. Almost anything can serve as a distraction for avoiding pain. The result is that nothing gets healed, and the pain and the emotional triggers continue to grow.

THINKING VS. FEELING

Thinking and feeling are distinct and separate approaches for relating to our environment, experiences, and memories.

"He who looks outside, dreams. He who looks inside awakens."

—Carl Jung

Thinking about and remembering what happened to us doesn't promote healing. That's where many of us get stuck. Real healing requires more than educating ourselves about narcissism or revisiting old memories. It takes more than adding new practices to our lives, like affirmations, meditation, or prayer. Those are all great for personal growth and for gaining insight, and I think it's beneficial to do any or all those things. But in my experience, by themselves, they're not enough to truly promote recovery from childhood trauma and abuse.

Here's my point: all of those are done on a *conscious* level.

Why You Have to Feel It

Healing emotional wounds of any kind can't be achieved using cognitive processes like thought, reasoning, and logic. It's not possible to "think" a feeling or an emotion. We must *feel* them. We can't "think" ourselves into a state of recovery, although using our cognitive abilities (such as reading, learning, and understanding) is absolutely a part of the process.

There's no way to make rational sense of your mother's behavior and trying to often leads to feeling the same kinds of pain, confusion, and frustration that we felt as kids. It's like running on the treadmill and expecting to get somewhere. We're surprised when we haven't gone anywhere, and we're exhausted from the effort. It's time to do the *feeling* part of the work. It's time to face the pain head-on, as an adult, and deal with what comes up. Be done with it once and for all.

Our emotional wounds don't live in our consciousness. They live in our *subconscious*.

It makes a tremendous amount of sense to tackle the damage where it lives, doesn't it? Our subconscious mind is "home" to our wounds. Recovery isn't possible if we avoid ourselves at this level

Facing and working through the memories brought me into and through the healing process. Looking directly at and re-experiencing the sorrow, confusion, and anger, but doing it this time as an adult, with an adult's perspective and understanding, knowing and feeling that, this time, I was safe.

If the idea of re-experiencing any part of your childhood frightens or concerns you, I encourage you to find a professional. Find an experienced, licensed abuse recovery expert. Look for counselors who work exclusively with narcissistic abuse survivors, Adult Children of

Alcoholics (ACA's), Adult Children of Narcissists (ACN's), or Complex-Post Traumatic Stress Disorder (C-PTSD) survivors.

Sometimes we've experienced so much of, or a particular kind of trauma, that we require the assistance of an experienced mental health professional. It helps to have another person lead the way and to validate our experiences; someone who's knowledgeable, experienced, professional, accepting, kind, loving, and who makes us feel safe.

There is courage and wisdom in seeking professional help.

Takeaways

- We have no idea what we'll discover along the way when we begin to recover.

- We can't put a time-frame on our recovery, set a calendar-goal or compare our progress to anyone else.

- Your healing journey is yours alone.

- Your healing journey will become a part of your life experience, and of you.

- Welcome whatever you discover.

Action for Healing

Using this list, check off the actions you have already started taking. Make an action plan and timeline for those you haven't started yet, and keep moving forward.

1. Examine, write about, and validate your childhood memories.

2. Examine and write about your feelings about narcissism.

3. Understand that your childhood circumstances were not your fault.

4. Awareness and understanding of at least 2 of your triggers and where they came from. Have a plan for the next time you're triggered.

5. Awareness of helping others, fixing their problems, offering advice, or removing their consequences, when they haven't asked you to do those things.

6. Experience with Narcissistic Awareness Grief, and it's impact on you. What stage are you currently in?

7. Examine whether you have been a target of projection and understand how your mother used projection to see her own unacceptable traits within you.

8. Examine whether you've witnessed the narcissistic abuse cycle in your own family. If so, which stage is the family in currently?

9. Examine some of the lies you were told as a child. Which ones do you still believe? Why or why not?

10. If you have experienced the silent treatment, understand how it impacted you.

11. Examine whether your family uses the rule, "Don't Talk, Don't Trust, Don't Feel," and understand how it impacts you.

12. Examine whether you've experienced feelings of shame and when it started. Read Brené Brown's materials on shame and vulnerability.

13. Examine whether you have been a source of narcissistic supply and how you contribute to that.

14. Examine whether you are in a trauma bond and how it's affecting you. Take steps to break the bond, such as practicing mindfulness. Mindfulness is one of the keys to healing.

15. Change your negative self-talk. That is also a major key to healing.

16. Examine and question your childhood beliefs and your thoughts and feelings connected to them.

17. Develop a list of actions you can take to protect yourself from, or avoid, a narcissistic rage.

18. Write about gaslighting episodes you remember.

19. Allow others the dignity and space to make and learn from their mistakes.

20. Have an outline to follow for conversations with your mother.

21. Set at least one personal boundary and enforced it.

22. Use the WEB method to identify potentially dangerous people.

Chapter Twenty-three
WHAT NOW?

"Sometimes it's not "answers" that hold the key to healing, but rather it's the understanding that who we are now is the result of all our past experiences, both the good and the bad."

After the initial devastation of recognizing our mother on the narcissistic spectrum, we may actually feel relieved. When we discover that maternal narcissism is a genuine "thing," that it has a *name*, that we are not alone, and that we are not crazy, it's an incredibly validating experience. I'll never forget the feelings of disbelief and shock, and then the slow dawning of *understanding* that overtook me as I processed this revelation. It was great to have information and understanding, but what was I supposed to do with it? How could knowing or understanding this *really help* me move forward?

You've broadened your understanding of narcissism, and you might even have a folder full of links, bookmarks, memes, and articles about Narcissistic Personality Disorder, toxic people, mental disorders, and the trauma they cause. You might even have a folder of recovery information. Good for you!

Learning is only the beginning. You'll also need to acknowledge and validate how narcissism affected you. If you feel comfortable, tell your story to someone you trust, someone who cares about your well-being, and supports you. You could do this through journaling, with a recovered, trust-worthy family member, emotionally stable friend, counselor, abuse recovery therapist, certified trauma recovery life-coach, C-PTSD specialist, or narcissist trauma support group.

Support groups are great for validating our feelings because the members have all had similar experiences. There is no judgment, shame, or anxiety about sharing those experiences. Everybody in the group is interested and motivated to recover and move forward.

Look at *all* the new information and the old memories without turning away. It's OK to be shocked, hurt, disappointed, and angry by the realization that your mother has narcissistic traits or is on the narcissistic spectrum. It's OK to realize you've been shortchanged. It's OK to acknowledge that your childhood could have been different. Your adult life could have been very different, too, if your mother had been emotionally stable and able to care for you properly. It's more than OK to feel everything you're feeling. We all get hurt, sometimes because of our own decisions, and sometimes because of other's choices or behavior. It's natural to feel wronged when someone mistreats us or hurts us.

We All Make Choices

You've begun to understand that the way you interact with your mother is a choice. Soon, you simply won't react to her when she's pushing your buttons. Instead, you'll respond calmly with grace and dignity.

Stop fantasizing about the kind of mother you wish she could've been or could *still* be. It's not going to happen. How long have you had this idea of how wonderful or loving it could be "if only......?" These thoughts will keep you stuck.

And most importantly: stop telling yourself that your mother will someday admit her hurtful behavior and apologize. Stop imagining the validation you'll feel when she finally realizes how much she's hurt you as she begins feeling remorse for her behavior.

A narcissistic mother believes she's never wrong, never does anything hurtful, never makes mistakes. She can't feel guilty because to feel guilt, she'd have to take responsibility for her actions, admit her transgression, and feel remorseful. But a narcissistic mom *justifies* her actions or blames someone for them. It's never her fault; it's always someone else's. The sooner you accept that she doesn't feel guilt or remorse, and isn't going to apologize, the sooner you'll be able to move on.

I know what I've said is harsh. It's because I care about your recovery. I've *been* there, and I understand. I spent years trying, hoping, wishing, tippy-toeing around, allowing myself to be a doormat and dumping ground, a loyal puppy who did tricks on command in exchange for a crumb of affection. I compromised myself, in all kinds of ways, to try to interest her in participating in my life. I dreamed of doing mother-daughter activities like shopping or meeting for coffee. Laughing. Being light and carefree. Having fun. Going out to lunch or a movie. Normal, everyday stuff, ya know?

I imagined her joyful reactions to all my milestones and accomplishments, like when I won a scholarship, graduated with honors, became engaged, got married, announced my first pregnancy. I used to imagine going baby-gear shopping with her. How happy we would be, enjoying our time together and looking forward to the birth. I used to daydream about how her face would light up when my kids came into the room, and how she would scoop them up and smother them with kisses. In my imaginings, she would do all of the things that she didn't do with me. Boy, do I have an amazingly active imagination, or what? The fantasies remained fantasies.

I thought I could *make* it happen if only I did or said the right things or could get her attention long enough. I felt like I was doing backflips and spitting nickels to get her attention.

Then during my recovery, I had a revelation that it just wasn't possible to have that kind of relationship with her, and that realization hurt. A LOT. After some time, I accepted this understanding. I dropped the illusion of "what it could be like" and simply accepted what is. I dropped the campaign to deceive myself. When I did, I felt robbed of a childhood and deprived of a *real* mother who could do *real* "mother stuff," like be happy to see me, talk to me, kiss and hug me, and want to spend time with me. I felt cheated out of the years I spent focusing on her, all because I simply couldn't give up the belief that she would change. Hope springs eternal, doesn't it?

The admission of reality and dropping the ruse was a soul-crushing experience. I felt orphaned, and the grieving process was difficult and long. I got stuck. I didn't know how to move through it and actually *heal*. I had to find a way to deal with the resentment and anger.

"You cannot have a positive life with a negative mind."

——Joyce Meyer

So, you see, Dear Reader, the healing process can be complex and lengthy.

Some of us feel further traumatized by the realization that we didn't understand, at the time, that the treatment we endured was abusive. We might feel nauseated, enraged, guilty, ashamed, or numb, as we comprehend this.

And by the way: it's *very* hard to believe that a mother could be capable of doing the things that a narcissistic mother does, let alone that she could do them to her children. It's especially difficult and painful to acknowledge or accept that *your* mother did them to *you*. It's challenging to think of our mothers as abusers, isn't it? But when we attain this insight and call it what it is, we also begin questioning everything we think we know about her. I remember feeling like I didn't know what was genuine about my mother and what wasn't. I remember feeling like our whole relationship had been a charade of manipulation, mind-games, and control. It pretty much devastated me for a while.

Whatever you feel, don't judge yourself for feeling it. Accept what you feel, and know that you'll be OK. Expect to feel a wide range of emotions, and just let them come. Those feelings are there for a reason. You're safe. You're an adult now. Be kind to yourself and let yourself feel and process this dazzling and unbelievable information, knowing that you're safe.

Recovering from any type of trauma or abuse is a complicated process, mentally, emotionally, physically, and spiritually. But it can be done.

"You either walk inside your story and own it or you stand outside your story and hustle for your worthiness."

—Brené Brown

THE TIMELINE

Understand that in recovery and healing, there's no timeline. You can set parameters, but you can't force it. Healing takes as long as it takes.

Everyone on this journey is on their *own* unique path, and no two are alike. We may have support, and friends may accompany us now and then, but the trail is narrow. Even when we work with a therapist, we walk through the vastness of the dark, scary place called "healing" alone.

What we see, hear, learn, and do along the way in recovery becomes part of our life experience. These recovery experiences will change us as individuals, and we alone get to determine whether they'll be positive or negative changes.

It's important that we don't compare our recovery journey with someone else's. There is no competition. There is no comparison. This healing journey is exclusively for you. It's your time to acknowledge and recognize some hard truths. Healing is a gift we give to ourselves, to finally deal with the emotional pain, memories, and triggers, so we can be free of these influences once and for all.

When we're focused on recovery, we need to consciously set aside time, regularly, for doing the recovery work. It takes awareness, focus, and commitment to do this. I believe that the more structured we are, the more we will see and feel the healing taking place. We're all different, but that's how it worked for me.

If you're stuck in any one area of recovery, it's important to know that you need to nudge yourself forward and keep going. I got stuck, but I made myself continue reading, learning, and doing the work to get past it.

You may find yourself hesitating because you're anxious or fearful of the next steps. Or maybe you don't want to revisit or reexperience specific or unknown upsetting events. Maybe you don't want to find out what you'll feel or discover next. I think if that's true, then working with a professional would be something to consider strongly. A professional could help you identify ways to get unstuck. Sometimes a shift in attitude or perspective is what it takes. Or you might benefit from trying a new or different approach, whether that means a different form of therapy, different therapist, or adding additional treatment. Whatever it takes, I hope you do it.

Sometimes self-help is enough, but other times we need something more. Please give yourself the gift of working with a therapist if your progress has stalled. We owe it to ourselves to do everything we can to heal.

During the recovery process, you might feel tired, emotionally drained, or even exhausted. Personally, depending on the type and amount of work I did, I sometimes felt like I'd been hit by a truck. There were times I felt depressed or angry, and days when my eyes hurt from crying. You might feel like quitting; you might find yourself thinking thoughts like: forget it, it isn't working, nothing's happening except for remembering painful times that I don't want to remember. Based on my own experience, all of those are signs that I was actually making progress. For me, the only way *out* of the trauma was *through* the trauma. Trauma specialists agree on that principle.

The bottled-up emotions that we weren't allowed to express are still inside, demanding to be recognized and affirmed. Those feelings (or their effects) don't magically disappear just because years have gone by. They're still there, waiting to be acknowledged. They won't go away until we do that.

We alone experienced these events, and we alone retain the memories, even if others were living in the household with us. Healing *requires* the validation of our experiences and our memories. We didn't understand that at the time, and we survived. Give yourself the gift of validating what you survived. Believe your memories. Acknowledge that events happened the way you remember.

Healing isn't about eliminating symptoms, but rather addressing the root causes of the pain.

When we start working through the trauma, we can finally begin to acknowledge and process the feelings that we were never allowed to recognize or vocalize when we were kids. As recovering adults, we can do that and finally release them. Afterward, when we remember, we won't have those old, familiar, emotional reactions anymore because we worked *through* them.

"Remembering" is validation. "Feeling" is validation. We didn't get any kind of validation when we were kids living in an abusive environment. It's time to validate ourselves.

So, in my own journey, I recalled the memories, felt the confusion, anger, guilt, shame, humiliation, etc. and acknowledged that what I was re-experiencing really happened—no more gaslighting or denying. I had to bring it all back up into the open where I could look at it, sift through it and feel it all again one final time, the LAST time, and be *done* with it.

My heart remembered being that sad little girl who was *expected* to obey without question and care for her mother's emotional needs. I remembered what it was like to be that girl whose natural mental state was confusion and whose goal it was to understand her mother's behavior. To find the reasons why her mother was usually angry, dismissive, or ignoring, and wasn't interested in interacting with her.

If your heart validates your painful experiences, try to be grateful for that. Listen when your heart speaks to you.

You probably have questions, and you want answers.

I'm going to suggest something that helped me sort out my thoughts, feelings, and questions: write them down as they come. Refer to them as you go through the recovery process. I found that my perspective and attitude about my childhood, as well as about my mother, shifted throughout the process, as I acquired new information or gained fresh insight. Yours might change too.

In fact, as you heal, having "answers" may actually become irrelevant.

Sometimes it's not "answers" that hold the key to healing, but rather it's the understanding that who we are now is the result of *all* our past experiences, both the good and the bad. Going forward to nurture and care for our newly discovered selves, in ways that our mother never could, is what will determine who we are tomorrow and every day after that.

We are survivors.

Healing from any hurtful or toxic event depends heavily on your own attitude. How we feel about ourselves dramatically influences the entire recovery process.

Recovery from maternal narcissistic abuse includes replacing negative thoughts and beliefs with new ones. We need to learn new ways of coping with stress, getting rid of self-sacrificing behaviors, practicing excellent self-care, and surrounding ourselves with people who validate our daily experience.

For the rest of this chapter, I'll share the methods, tools, and techniques that I used to help me recover from the effects of maternal narcissistic abuse.

Keep in mind that I'm **not** saying that:

- my way is the *only* way to heal;

- you have to use all of these techniques;

- you have to use the methods in a specific order;

- you have to spend money;

- you'll get the same or better results;

- they'll work for you;

- I'm fully recovered. Recovery is a life-long process, and even so, relapses occur. Healing is a (lifelong) process, not an event.

Everyone is different. You had your own individual childhood experiences, and I had mine. I'm sharing my personal experiences with various healing methods to show what's available and what's possible. There are many other modalities out there that you may want to consider investigating.

My own healing journey began in the 1980s. The process was not straightforward or linear, and there was no specific methodology. It was more like exploring possibilities and trying new approaches as they became available to me. I felt that doing something was better than doing nothing, and if a particular approach didn't work for me, I was OK with that.

A Few More Thoughts

Any recovery work requires the willingness to be open to new ideas about self-love, self-respect, personal growth, self-acceptance, and even forgiveness.

Healing doesn't mean cutting yourself off from your mother. Going "no contact" can be an aspect of the healing process but does not promote healing by itself. Healing requires a willingness to do the work to become a new and better version of ourselves.

Looking directly at and re-experiencing the anguish, anger, confusion, and isolation head-on—with adult perspective and strength—is empowering. We would never have been able to do that as children.

I've mentioned support groups a lot. There are online support groups too. I've seen some that were top-notch and effective, and I've seen online groups that were exploitive, used to focus on negative thoughts and feelings, and erroneously spread false information and confusion. When appropriate measures are in place, such as having a moderator and group rules for posting, negativity can be kept to a minimum, and everyone can stay focused on healing. Under the right circumstances, online support groups can be very useful for making new connections, learning new information, and finding helpful resources.

GETTING STARTED

While it's daunting to figure out how to begin the recovery process, I suggest that you keep an open mind, do your research, and experiment with different approaches to see what works best for you.

The first thing is to let yourself grieve the loss of the childhood and mother you never got to have.

You'll have good days and not-so-good ones. I can tell you from experience that you'll want to give up at times. You might feel you aren't making progress or that it's not worth it because of how painful and difficult it can be.

However, you should give any method a reasonable chance. Nothing works overnight. Be fair to yourself by allowing your methodology to have a real effect and make a difference.

For my personal healing journey, I used the eleven methods described below. In retrospect, I think the order in which these take place is probably an important consideration, but I didn't have a choice at the time I began my recovery process. There was no discussion of "maternal narcissistic abuse," or Narcissistic Abuse Syndrome, and as I mentioned, I was considered an ACA, which was also a pretty new concept. There was little research and few treatment options available. When I began my healing journey, it was kind of a hit-or-miss approach. Today there are specific methodologies for abuse and trauma recovery facilitated by experts in their fields.

As you heal, finding "answers" may actually become irrelevant to you. It's not "answers" that hold the key to healing, but rather the understanding that who we are today is the result of all of our past experiences.

Each of the methods I used, listed below, overlapped to some extent. I didn't use them serially or stop using one when I began another. Once I determined that a technique worked for me, I continued using it in combination with others that also worked. I still use these methods today whenever I need them. They help reduce stress, calm my fight-or-flight response, and help me cope when I'm triggered.

Journaling—The writing exercises at the end of each chapter are a good start for healing. Sorting through confusing memories, negative thoughts, or outdated beliefs about yourself allows you to look at past experiences with an adult perspective. It enables you to validate your memories in a way that wasn't done before. As you work through this book and do the journaling work, you'll most likely begin uncovering thoughts, memories, and beliefs you've probably carried since childhood. You'll likely notice patterns of behavior, yours and those of others, as well as your methods of coping. You may become aware of recurrent relationship themes and old, outdated, or irrelevant examples of self-talk. Uncovering and discovering these will be useful in the next steps for producing real change.

If you're interested in using the **Lemon Moms Companion Workbook** *instead of journaling, it's available for purchase on Amazon.com*

Identifying and changing beliefs—Finding the origins of dysfunctional and hurtful beliefs (for example, "I'm not good enough," "I'm not lovable," "I'm not worthy") requires us to look deeply and fearlessly within ourselves. It begins with mindfulness, self-observation, and noticing the belief when it occurs. Questioning the validity of these beliefs and replacing them is a foundational aspect of healing. A Google search will reveal a lot of results about discovering and eliminating hurtful beliefs. There are do-it-yourself methods and online courses, as well as face-to-face counseling programs. Using these, you can learn to identify limiting or untrue ideas about yourself and purge and replace them with new, healthier ones. Personally, I found the Emotional Freedom Technique (EFT) to work very well for changing faulty beliefs. EFT is explained further in number six of this list.

Cognitive behavior therapy (CBT)—CBT is a goal-oriented talk therapy that uses a practical approach to problem-solving. It takes place with a mental health professional in a structured setting, with a limited number of sessions because it's a short-term treatment. CBT is useful for developing an awareness of inaccurate or negative thinking and for learning new ways of viewing challenging situations and responding. It focuses on one's thoughts, beliefs, attitudes, and behavior, and it can be combined with other treatments. (Mayo Clinic, Cognitive behavioral therapy 2019).

Positive affirmations—These are frequently repeated, affirmative statements intended to change behavior, thinking, and habits. The specific vocabulary used in an affirmation prompts inspirational and motivational feelings; for example, repeating "It's simple and easy to be successful" will positively influence one's ideas about success. Using affirmational statements can reprogram thinking patterns over time and also lower the effects of stress. With repetition, the messages become fixed in the subconscious mind, helping to produce desired changes. Scientific evidence attests to the effectiveness of positive affirmations. A study done in 2013 found that performing a short affirmational exercise raised the problem-solving abilities of "chronically stressed" test—subjects to the same level as those with low-stress levels (Creswell et al. 2013). Another study done in 2016 found that a stronger sense of self-worth led to an improved sense of well-being (Cascio et al. 2016).

Sensorimotor therapy—Sensorimotor techniques engage the body and mind simultaneously in the recovery process. This type of therapy calms the limbic system by teaching awareness of bodily responses pertaining to healing. I didn't work with a sensorimotor practitioner, but doing so is an option for you. Instead, I used similar, related, therapeutic approaches to calm my limbic system, such as listening to soothing music, meditating, massages, deep breathing, hatha yoga, and low impact exercise like bike riding, dancing, and walking.

Emotional freedom technique (EFT)—I love this technique. The emotional freedom technique is based on the premise that when emotions become attached to thoughts, a belief is formed.

With EFT, we can change feelings and beliefs.

When we perform EFT, we "tap" on several nerve-channels, "energy meridians," which are located around the body. Energy meridians, a theory in Chinese medicine, are channels throughout the body where blockages of stuck feelings can cause sickness or poor health. Tapping on a meridian sends little shockwaves to reset the flow of energy, moving stuck energy along. We don't know where the particular feeling is actually "stuck," so we tap on several of the meridian tapping-points. The feeling gets cleared, which breaks the attachment to the thought, and destroys the belief. Now the thought can be re-processed and re-examined objectively without feeling any emotion. The thought can be replaced with a new thought, and if a feeling becomes attached to the new thought, wow, we'll have a whole new belief too.

"A belief is a thought that we are emotionally attached to."

—Magnus Dell

When I used EFT, it was during a planned, uninterrupted weekend during which I spent several hours systematically tapping through each painful memory that arose. Afterward, I was exhausted and emotionally drained. But it worked. Today I can think about past traumatic experiences and no longer respond emotionally. It's freeing to be able to talk about those events matter-of-factly without an emotional reaction. There are EFT practitioners out there, but I learned everything I needed to use the technique successfully from http://www.tapping.com/.

Neuro-linguistic programming (NLP)—This is a user-friendly way to change thinking patterns and reframe memories. NLP focuses on the "how" instead of the "why." It uses the connection between mind (neuro) and language (linguistic) to change thoughts and behavior (programming). NLP combines visualization and verbal narrative (Neuro-Linguistic Programming). This combination tells the brain to "see" memories differently, and this changes the feelings connected with the memories.

It felt a little silly at first, imagining my inner critic with a silly voice as it recited my negative self-talk. And replaying painful memories in black and white on my inner "movie screen" as they shrank in size and floated away seemed a bit weird. But I discovered that with an open mind and plenty of repetition, NLP had a positive effect in reducing the intensity and meaningfulness of certain events.

Inner child work and reparenting (ICW)—both of these methods reduce the guilt, shame, fear, hatred, self-loathing, and anger associated with traumatic childhood events. Each entails a process of acknowledging, contacting, understanding, accepting, and healing your "inner child," your original self. Your inner child is where joy, awe, innocence, sensitivity, and playfulness are experienced. When you do this type of healing work, you'll speak to your inner child, look at pictures of yourself as a child, rediscover activities that you enjoyed as a child, and take "journeys" together via meditation and visualization. By working with your inner child, you can grieve and heal the trauma together.

Reparenting is an extension of inner child work. It involves loving your inner child unconditionally, along with supporting, protecting, and nurturing. When you reparent, you help your inner child understand past painful events, set boundaries, improve self-confidence, and develop a sense of self.

Al-Anon—Al-Anon is a free support group, and fellowship that uses an adapted version of the twelve-step values of Alcoholics Anonymous (A.A.). Swiss psychiatrist Carl Jung, in the 1920s, was interested in treating and understanding alcoholism. He said that sobriety could be achieved through "higher education of the mind beyond the confines of mere rationalism." This influenced the spiritual aspect of Alcoholics Anonymous.

Since my first treatment was as an Adult Child of an Alcoholic, it made sense to try Al-Anon. Al-Anon serves families and friends of alcoholics, providing support for those affected by the dysfunctional behavior resulting from someone's alcoholism. It follows a twelve-step format using a cognitive-behavioral approach in each step, addressing codependency, boundaries, self-talk, self-esteem, parenting, trust, denial, relationships, and countless more issues.

There are many twelve-step programs, and each addresses specific dysfunctions, such as drug addiction, eating disorders, and sexual dysfunction. Find out more at https://sobernation.com/list-of-12-step-programs/

Loving detachment—When we get used to healthy practices (such as boundary-setting), we start to develop new perspectives and attitudes, and feel differently about ourselves and others. For the first time, we may see ourselves as autonomous individuals. Our separateness and uniqueness begin to be positive and valuable attributes. We begin to recognize our strengths and use our personal power. The responsibility for other's feelings, or for fixing their problems, disappears. We learn that we have needs of our own and that they're our primary focus. It starts to make sense that "connection" requires us to be proactive in reaching out. At that point, we begin to trust, and we also become willing to be vulnerable, taking the risk to share our individual stories. And all of these take us to the concept of loving detachment.

When I first heard the term, I thought I knew what it meant. I was very familiar with detachment, and I knew how to do that when I needed to. But what I didn't understand was that there are different styles of detachment, and the method I used and was most familiar with was actually not a form of *loving* detachment. I had a lot to learn.

Detachment sounds negative, doesn't it? How can detaching from someone be loving? If you're confused, I can help. Let me start by telling you what loving detachment is not.

Practicing loving detachment isn't mean, harsh, or selfish; instead, it's compassionate and kind. In short, loving detachment is a type of healthy boundary. According to Al-Anon, loving detachment means "caring enough about others to allow them to learn from their mistakes. It also means being responsible for our own welfare and making decisions without ulterior motives or the desire to control others."

I didn't learn how to lovingly detach until I learned about codependency and how to set healthy boundaries. Even after becoming familiar with the idea of detaching, actually doing it was anxiety-provoking; I was out of my comfort zone. So when opportunities presented themselves for practicing loving detachment, I decided to take them, and I gradually became comfortable using this new tool as a form of self-care.

Lovingly detaching means choosing to distance yourself *emotionally* from a situation and its' consequences. We take the focus off of the other person and put it squarely on ourselves. We understand that the other person is entitled to make their own choices, including the choice to hurt us. They're also entitled to deal with the results of those choices. So while we feel compassion for them, we focus on *ourselves, and we feel at peace about whatever happens next.*

Loving detachment is judgment-free. Detaching, in this way, allows us to intellectually and compassionately separate the person from their behavior. We can now see that the person and their behavior are two separate things. We can choose to love the person and feel compassion for them while despising their behavior.

When we lovingly detach from our mothers, we stop focusing on her, and we don't take responsibility for her actions or their consequences any longer.

Detaching with love from my mother means that I listen instead of offering unsolicited advice. I don't rush in to fix problems. If we disagree, I don't argue or try to change her position; I state my opinion, and I accept that she's entitled to have her own. We don't have to agree. I no longer ask, "What can I do to help?" and "How can I make it better?" I don't steal her personal power, and I leave her the dignity to address her own problems. If she instigates, I don't pick up my end of the tug-of-war rope; instead, I might end our conversation. This means that I disconnect emotionally when she's being mean or stirring the pot. I let go of my desire to control her or the outcomes and focus on the next best thing for me. None of these approaches are mean; they focus on letting her run her own life and solve her own problems while I take care of me, my life, and solve my own problems too.

As with boundary-setting, there is no need to discuss your requirement to detach or to get permission, and your mother does not need to agree to it.

When I feel the need to detach, I find it necessary to first accept and validate my thoughts and my feelings. Next, I commit to maintaining my focus and productivity by *not* concentrating on my mother. Doing these things puts me in the right frame of mind to successfully detach with love. There's no anger, no fear, no need to go numb, or to be indifferent. It's like what my teacher friends say to their students: "Keep your eyes on your own paper." I commit to keeping my eyes on my own needs, my own life, and focus on my own work. There's nothing mean about that. When we view loving detachment from this perspective, we can clearly see that it's not a form of running away; it's a way of running *toward* ourselves. Loving detachment helps us break free of codependent behaviors by reminding us that we're separate people, with our own likes, needs, goals, choices, and consequences of our own.

Practicing loving detachment requires knowing how to set boundaries and a decent measure of self-esteem and self-worth. Do the work required.

THE HALT METHOD OF SELF-CARE

When our basic needs aren't met, our capacity to think rationally and logically is affected. When we take care of ourselves, life feels better, and we feel good about ourselves. Our beliefs about what we should hang onto and what we should let go of start to shift, and we start setting healthy boundaries. We begin to comprehend better what's our responsibility and what's not.

To get there, we need to start with self-awareness and a mindful approach. The HALT method (Al-Anon Acronyms) is a quick and easy way of checking in with ourselves at the moment, to see what we need.

The acronym HALT stands for hungry, angry, lonely, and tired.

Self-care and mindfulness go hand in hand. You can't know what you need if you're not paying attention to yourself or your own life. You can't take good care of yourself if you're preoccupied with someone else's needs. When you're HALTed, give yourself what you need to take care of yourself. Remember, good self-care should be moving higher on your priority list.

Hungry—Hunger can be a sign that you lack or need something to eat, or it can be emotional hunger. If you're hungry for food, ask yourself: Is my stomach growling? Am I irritable or lightheaded? When was the last time I ate? Physical hunger is associated with food, diet, and nutrition, which are undeniably important aspects of our overall health. We require nourishing food to feel well and to thrive. Take a look at how and what you're eating and see if there's room for improvement.

Maybe you're feeling emotional hunger. Ask yourself: Am I craving attention, validation, affection, or affirmation? Stop and do a quick self-assessment to figure out what you need. If it's validation, validate yourself. If it's an affirmation, affirm yourself. If it's attention or affection, find ways to give those to yourself. We can't rely on others to meet all of our needs. Meeting our needs is our responsibility.

Angry—When we're angry, our brain is flooded with chemicals that activate our fight-or-flight response. So, it's easy to overreact, and when we do, our behavior might be out of proportion to the actual event that triggered it. Anger is a *secondary* emotion, meaning that there is always an emotion we feel first, for a fraction of a second, and that *first* (primary) emotion triggers the anger. So when you're angry, it's essential to stop and figure out the primary emotion that triggered your anger. For example, maybe you felt ignored, belittled, or insulted, and *that* triggered your outrage.

Lonely—When we feel alone, it's often because we think we don't fit in or belong, or that people won't accept us or understand us. Sometimes we withdraw because we fear criticism, judgment, or even worse, rejection.

Loneliness leads to isolation, and isolation is often a maladaptive coping mechanism. Trying to fix loneliness by using self-destructive behaviors like drinking, binge-eating, shopping, or gambling doesn't solve the problem. Those behaviors will just create new problems. The cure for isolation (and loneliness) is to be willing to be vulnerable and to reach out to others and make a connection.

Tired—When we're tired or sleepy, we're incredibly vulnerable to making poor choices because our brains aren't functioning optimally. Maintaining healthy sleep cycles and routines is essential for both physical and mental health.

When we're sleep-deprived, it's not time to make decisions or have meaningful conversations. If you find yourself tired and you have a meeting to attend or a decision to make, postpone it if possible until you're better-rested.

HALT a way of setting healthy boundaries and a straightforward way to alert us to pay attention to our own self-care. When we feel HALTed, it means we need to give ourselves attention and address an unmet need. We must stop what we're doing and take care of that unmet need as a priority.

When we ignore our needs, we create an unhealthy emotional environment in which it's impossible to thrive. When we're in that unhealthy place, we tend to think negatively, fail to see choices, make poor decisions, forget, withdraw, and push people away. We may even stop enforcing our personal boundaries or lapse back into codependent behaviors. Neglecting ourselves to take care of someone capable of their own self-care can actually make us ill. Pay attention to what your body is telling you and then redirect the focus back onto yourself.

Remember that airline mandate about putting on your *own* oxygen mask *before* attempting to help others with theirs? In the same spirit, ensure that your self-care commitments are at least as valuable to you as someone else's would be. If you don't take care of you, then who will? No one is capable of caring more about you than *you* are.

It's OK to realize you've been shortchanged. It's OK to acknowledge that your childhood could have been different. Your adult life could have been very different, too, if your mother had been emotionally stable and able to care for you properly. It's more than OK to feel everything you're feeling.

Chapter Twenty-four
A NEW BEGINNING

"Healing may not be so much about getting better, as about letting go of everything that isn't you—all of the expectations, all of the beliefs—and becoming who you are."

—Rachel Naomi Remen

Using the techniques and resources in this book, you can start to heal.

Below are some indications that you've begun to heal. This list is by no means complete. Feel free to add your own healing indicators, whether you've already accomplished them or if they're goals for the future.

INDICATORS OF RECOVERY:

- You're beginning to respect yourself.

- You've set some new boundaries.

- You focus more on what makes you happy and what's important to you rather than making others happy or knowing what's important to them.

- You've found activities that you love, and you do them regularly.

- You're in touch with your intuition, and you're learning to trust it.

- You realize it's not your job, and it never was your job, to treat or fix your mother or anyone else.

- You've examined your childhood programming, questioned each of the misperceptions you were expected to believe about yourself, and are working on letting go of your mother's faulty perceptions of you.

- You're creating new ideas about who you are, based on how far you've come and who you are today.

- When you see narcissistic behavior, you recognize it for what it is, and you steer clear.

- You're learning to fulfill your own needs, and you don't feel guilty about it.

- You recognize that your mother has a problem with thinking and perceiving and that she'll probably never address it.

- You understand that the crazy-making feelings you had around your mother were a normal reaction to her abnormal behavior. Your brain was functioning precisely the way it was supposed to, to protect and help you try to make sense of a situation that would never make sense.

- You're aware of when you're self-gaslighting, and you stop as soon as you become aware.

- You feel grounded and safe most of the time.

- You're getting comfortable having difficult conversations.

- You're getting comfortable confronting people who need to be confronted.

- You stand up for yourself, calmly and confidently.

- You are fiercely on your own side.

- A person's character and integrity matter more to you than their popularity, sense of humor, success, or physical attributes.

- You're not interested in continuing people-pleasing behaviors.

- You like yourself much of the time.

- You're aware of your self-talk, and make sure that it's positive.

- You focus more often on what makes you happy and what is important to you.

- You're developing personal values.

- You're working through your anger.

- You're working on forgiveness.

- You're learning to allow others to earn your trust.

- You notice when "red flags" are present. When it's not possible to avoid those individuals, you maintain low-contact and enforce your boundaries.

- You're doing recovery work on a regular basis and acknowledging your progress.

- You believe that you're a strong person.

- You're educating yourself about narcissism, toxic people, and toxic relationships.

- You're creating new beliefs about yourself based on who you've become and who you are becoming.

- You've begun to prioritize self-care in its many forms.

- You seek out and practice guided meditations that help you feel positive, strong, and peaceful.

- You journal.

- You no longer acquiesce to people or events that intrude on your plans, privacy, safety, or serenity.

- You don't worry about whether your life choices will make your mother angry or upset. You're making life choices that are all about *you* now.

- When a narcissist invites you to an argument, you decline. ☺

- You're aware of relationships that take advantage of you.

- You focus on solutions, not problems.

- You're more concerned about your life than anyone else's.

- You no longer tolerate people who devalue or disrespect you. You kick them out of your life, and you feel good about doing it.

- You're becoming your own advocate.

- You're beginning to know what's good for you and what isn't.

- You're no longer willing to accept someone else's version of reality.

- You're not willing to minimize your education, talents, skills, or abilities in order to accommodate someone else's personal insecurities.

- You're not willing to minimize your education, talents, skills, or abilities in order to accommodate someone else's faulty perception of you.

- You know when you're being manipulated by guilt, shame, passive-aggressive behavior, and other forms of control, and you no longer let yourself be controlled.

- You're getting comfortable with communicating about the things that you will and won't accept and/or do in your relationships.

- You recognize when you're being gaslighted and refuse to let your reality be re-written by someone else.

- You'll absolutely leave situations that make you feel uncomfortable or unsafe.

- You feel worthy of being seen and heard.

- You're uncomfortable when you're in denial, and you recognize it for what it is.

- You recognize that you are a complete person, and you don't need validation or acceptance from anyone except yourself.

- You don't need permission to exist.

- You're no longer interested in being a people-pleaser, and you understand and accept that this kind of enabling behavior makes you a potential victim.

- You refuse to give up your own plans or dreams to achieve somebody else's.

- You refuse to spend your precious time doing things you don't want to do that might gain someone's attention, affection, approval, or love.

- You've decided to stop over-functioning.

- You've decided to stop "rowing the boat" all by yourself. You understand and believe that others need to do their share of the work.

- You say "no" more often and set limits for others' behavior and expectations.

- You understand that there are consequences for every action, and you let others deal with their own consequences.

- You recognize that all relationships are two-way interactions.

- You no longer make excuses for or minimize someone else's behavior.

- You don't tolerate "walking on eggshells.".

- You empathize, but you draw the line at being taken advantage of.

- You realize that boundaries work two ways: you no longer violate others' boundaries by rescuing, or trying to fix them or their circumstances.

- You ask for clarification when you're confused by something someone says or does.

- You're getting comfortable disengaging from toxic people, and you know when and why it's necessary.

- You recognize that people who use mind-games, manipulation, secrecy, intimidation, hurtful sarcasm or teasing, are toxic individuals, and you enforce the boundaries that protect you.

- You see that praise, flattery, compliments, or charm can be subtle forms of manipulation, and those simply don't work on you anymore.

- You're not willing to stay in a relationship that makes you feel drained, confused, or doubtful of your sanity or your self-worth.

- You don't tolerate others crossing your personal boundaries or talking about: your appearance, weight, relationships, or achievements.

- You accept yourself in all your imperfection.

- You understand that "perfection" doesn't exist, and that your vulnerabilities, strengths, and weaknesses all combine to create the complete and lovable person you are.

- You trust your decision-making abilities, and you make decisions more easily.

Once you begin your healing program, you'll start to notice some changes in the ways that you think, perceive, and feel. The order in which the changes occur is irrelevant, and the changes are entirely unique to each recovering individual. You'll start healing where and when you need to, on your own exclusive timetable.

Those of us who've been affected by maternal narcissism need to heal and reclaim our emotional balance, sense of self, and well-being. To recover, we must go through each stage of NAG, eliminate codependency, and set healthy boundaries. When we heal, we live above and beyond our fabricated childhood reality.

"When we're defined by what people think, we lose the courage to be vulnerable. Therefore, we need to be selective about the feedback we let into our lives. For me, if you're not in the arena getting your ass kicked, I'm not interested in your feedback."

—Brené Brown

I wish you continued healing and the gift of lifelong self-improvement and self-care.

Glossary of Terms

Adverse Childhood Experiences (ACEs): are certain kinds of traumatic events that occur during childhood before the age of 18. When children experience trauma and educators can understand its impact, trauma-informed interventions may be developed that lessen the resulting negative consequences.

Amygdala: an almond-shaped structure in the brain involved with experiencing emotions. There are two, one on each side of the brain.

Boundaries: protect us from someone else's behavior or from engaging in activities that we'd rather not. Setting healthy boundaries protect and empower us regarding our safety, emotional stability, and mental health.

Codependent (enabler): an individual with an emotional and behavioral illness affecting their ability to have healthy, mutually satisfying relationships. Codependency is a learned behavior, so it's passed down through generations. It occurs when a person supports or enables another person's addiction, mental illness, immaturity, irresponsibility, or under-achievement. Codependents rely on others for a sense of identity, approval, or affirmation. They are "people-pleasers" who willingly play by the "rules" of others losing their own identity in the process.

Cognitive dissonance: the mental discomfort experienced from holding two or more contradictory beliefs, ideas, or values.

Cognitive empathy: having the *intellectual* understanding that someone is feeling a particular emotion, but not feeling anything in response to that awareness.

Complex-Post-traumatic Stress Disorder (C-PTSD): results from a series of trauma causing events, or one prolonged event, whereas PTSD is usually related to a single traumatic event. Complex-Post-traumatic Stress Disorder can be the result of narcissistic abuse. Common symptoms include flashbacks, panic attacks, nightmares, overactive startle response, habitually thinking about the traumatic event.

Diagnostic and Statistical Manual (DSM): a publication by the American Psychiatric Association used by clinicians to classify and diagnose mental disorders in children and adults. There have been several iterations of the DSM, the most recent of these completed in 2013, and known as the fifth edition or DSM-5 (DSM-V).

Dissociation: losing the sense of "who I am, where I am, or of what I'm doing." It's a protective response that allows emotional separation from trauma or abuse as it's happening.

Emotional Freedom Technique (EFT): an intervention that involves tapping on endpoints of "energy meridians" located around the body, to reduce tension, deepen the mind-body connection, and manage symptoms of anxiety, depression, or stress.

Ego: the part of the mind that arbitrates between the conscious and the unconscious. It's responsible for our sense of self, personal identity and is the filter through which we see ourselves. We tell our egos specific "stories" in order to continue living with certain self-defining beliefs.

Emotional empathy: the ability to put ourselves in another person's place and feel the emotions they're feeling.

Empathy gene: referred to in a study published March 12, 2018, in the journal *Translational Psychiatry*, and the most extensive genetic study of empathy to date. It found that "how empathetic" we are is partly due to genetics. —University of Cambridge

Enabling: taking responsibility, blame, or making excuses for a person's harmful or hurtful behavior. Also known as Codependency.

Enmeshment: occurs when personal boundaries between two or more people are unclear. There is no delineation of "what's mine" and "what's yours" in terms of personal responsibility.

Fight or flight: describes the quickly occurring release of hormones that activate a body's ability to deal with danger or threats. During this process, the sympathetic nervous system stimulates the adrenal glands, triggering the release of adrenaline and noradrenaline, hormones that increase heart rate, blood pressure, and breathing rate. It takes 20 to 60 minutes for the body to return to its baseline level of functioning.

Gaslighting: a tactic used to gain power and control over an individual by prompting them to doubt their senses or memory. The goal of gaslighting is to cause someone to question their reality and doubt their memory and judgment.

Gray rock: a way of encouraging an emotionally unbalanced person to lose interest by training them to view you as uninteresting or boring.

Hippocampus: a brain structure located under the cerebral cortex, and part of the limbic system. It plays a vital role in moving information from short-term to long-term memory.

Loving detachment: means "caring enough about others to allow them to learn from their mistakes. It also means being responsible for our own welfare and making decisions without ulterior motives or the desire to control others." -Al-Anon literature

Mixed message: a type of communication where an individual gives conflicting information, either verbal or non-verbal.

Narcissistic injury: anything a narcissist perceives as a threat to their 'false self' or their sense of importance and dominance.

Narcissistic Personality Disorder (NPD): a disorder recognized by the DSM, characterized by these nine criteria:

1. grandiose sense of self-importance

2. preoccupied with fantasies of unlimited success, power, beauty, etc.

3. believes s/he is 'special' and can only be understood by, or associate with like-minded people

4. requires excessive admiration

5. feels entitled to, and expects special treatment

6. manipulative and exploitative

7. lacks empathy

8. envious of others and/or believes others are envious of them

9. arrogant or haughty behavior.

To be diagnosed with narcissism, at least five of these specific traits must be expressed.

Narcissistic rage: intense anger, aggression, or passive-aggression displayed by a narcissist when they experience a setback or challenges their illusion of grandiosity, entitlement, or superiority, triggering their inadequacy, shame, and/or vulnerability. –Psychology Today, July 8, 2018

Narcissistic supply (NS): a concept introduced into psychoanalytic theory by Otto Fenichel in 1938, describing a type of admiration and support that a narcissist takes from their environment. It is essential to their self-esteem.

No contact (NC): an example of a boundary, used to prevent recurring abuse. It is usually considered to be a "last resort" for protection against dysfunctional or abusive behavior.

Passive-aggression: involves showing aggression in a passive, more socially acceptable way.

Projection: the attribution of a trait we dislike in ourselves onto someone else.

Reaction: a reciprocal or counteracting force, typically quick, without much thought. Aggressive.

Response: a thoughtful, calm, and non-threatening reply.

Scapegoating: a practice seen in dysfunctional families. The scapegoat is the person who gets blamed for offenses and injustices that happen to family members, and the role can be temporary or permanent. Family members other than the narcissistic mom take turns in the scapegoat role. The mom determines the scapegoat.

Self-avoid: behavior that helps avoid or escape particular thoughts or feelings. It can involve "doing" or "not doing" something. –Psychology Today, March 5, 2013

Self-gaslighting: a form of self-doubt and self-deception that contributes to maintaining codependency. It's a consequence of accepting continual blame or living in a dysfunctional environment with inadequate emotional support.

Silent treatment: a way to inflict pain without causing visible marks. Research shows that "ignoring" or "excluding" someone activates the part of the brain where physical pain is experienced.

Trauma bond: powerful emotional bonds that are created between two individuals undergoing cycles of abuse together. Over time trauma bonds become very resistant to change, and a codependent relationship develops.

Triangulation: the manipulation of a relationship between two people by a third person controlling the amount and type of communication between them. It is used to generate rivalry between the two parties, as a way to "divide and conquer."

Triggering: reacting to old, buried memories with a knee-jerk, unconscious behavior. Triggers indicate unhealed wounds.

Validation: the act of recognizing or affirming someone's feelings or thoughts as sound or worthwhile. Validation is an essential aspect of mothering because it contributes to effective and safe communication. Feeling heard and understood leads to feelings of trust, a cornerstone of every relationship.

Virtue signaling: the not so humble announcement of one's character traits, moral views, or values.

References

Ainsworth, M. D. S., & Bell, S. M. (1970). Attachment, exploration, and separation: Illustrated by the behavior of one-year-olds in a strange situation. *Child Development*, 41(1), 49. doi: 10.2307/1127388.

American Psychiatric Association. *Alternative DSM-5 model for personality disorders*. Fifth Edition. Washington, DC: American Psychiatric Publishing, Inc; 2013. 761-81.

Atkinson, A. (n.d.). *How adult children of narcissists can begin to heal*. Retrieved June 7, 2019, from https://queenbeeing.com/two-faced-identifying-parental-narcissism/

Atkinson, Angela (2015). *Take back your life: 103 highly-effective strategies to snuff out a narcissist's gaslighting and enjoy the happy life you really deserve* .

Baskin-Sommers, A., Krusemark, E., & Ronningstam, E. (2014, July). *Empathy in Narcissistic Personality Disorder: from clinical and empirical perspectives*. Retrieved July 10, 2019, from https://www.ncbi.nlm.nih.gov/pmc/articles/PMC4415495/.

Bowlby, J. (1969). *Attachment and loss*. London: Hogarth Press.

Boyes, A. (2013, January 17). 50 *Common cognitive distortions*. Retrieved August 2, 2019, from https://www.psychologytoday.com/us/blog/in-practice/201301/50-common-cognitive-distortions.

Brenner, Grant Hilary. (2018, September 9) *"Is projection the most powerful defense mechanism?"* Psychology Today, Sussex Publishers. Retrieved August 12, 2019, from www.psychologytoday.com/us/blog/experimentations/201809/is-projection-the-most-powerful-defense-mechanism.

Bressert, S. (2019, March 19). *Dependent personality disorder symptoms.* Retrieved July 7, 2019, from https://psychcentral.com/disorders/dependent-personality-disorder/symptoms/.

Bressert, S. (2019, April 20). *Narcissistic Personality Disorder: symptoms & treatments.* Retrieved August 17, 2019, from https://psychcentral.com/disorders/narcissistic-personality-disorder/.

Brown, Brené. (2008). I thought it was just me (but it isn't): making the journey from "what will people think" to "I am enough." New York: Gotham Books.

Burgo, Joseph. The narcissist you know: defending yourself against extreme narcissists in an all-about-me age. New York: Touchstone, 2016.

Caligor, E., Levy, K. N., & Yeomans, F. E. (2015). Narcissistic Personality Disorder: Diagnostic and clinical challenges. *American Journal of Psychiatry*, 172(5), 415–422. doi: 10.1176/appi.ajp.2014.14060723

Caligor, E., & Petrini, M. J. (2018). *Narcissistic personality disorder: Epidemiology, pathogenesis, clinical manifestations, course, assessment, and diagnosis.* Retrieved November 18, 2019, from https://www.uptodate.com/contents/narcissistic-personality-disorder-epidemiology-pathogenesis-clinical-manifestations-course-assessment-and-diagnosis.

Carnes, P. J. (2016). *Trauma bonding using real life examples.* Retrieved December 28, 2019, from https://reachcounseling.com/trauma-informed-symposium-2017-presenter-materials/trauma-bonding-using-real-life-examples-marissa-ghavami/.

Carnes, P., & Phillips, B. D. (2019). *The betrayal bond: breaking free of exploitive relationships*. Deerfield Beach, FL: Health Communications, Inc.

Cascio, C.N., Brook O'Donnell, M., Tinney, F.J., Lieberman, M.D., Taylor, S.E., Strecher, V.J., Falk, E.B. Self-affirmation activates brain systems associated with self-related processing and reward and is reinforced by future orientation, *Social Cognitive and Affective Neuroscience*, Volume 11, Issue 4, April 2016, Pages 621–629, https://doi.org/10.1093/scan/nsv136.

Centers for Disease Control and Prevention. (2016). *About the CDC-Kaiser ACE study: Major findings*. Retrieved June 2, 2019, from https://www.cdc.gov/violenceprevention/acestudy/about.html.

Centers for Disease Control and Prevention (2019, April 9). *About Adverse Childhood Experiences* |Violence Prevention|Injury Center|CDC. Retrieved May 5, 2019, from https://www.cdc.gov/violenceprevention/childabuseandneglect/acestudy/aboutace.html.

Cherry, K. (2019, September 18). *How to understand and identify passive-aggressive behavior*. Retrieved October 18, 2019, from https://www.verywellmind.com/what-is-passive-aggressive-behavior-2795481.

Cole, T. (2019, August 15). *Scapegoat, Golden Child & More: How to identify & heal from narcissistic family roles*. Retrieved December 2, 2019, from https://www.terricole.com/narc-family-roles/.

Creswell, J. D., Dutcher, J. M., Klein, W. M. P., Harris, P. R., & Levine, J. M. (2013). Self-affirmation improves problem-solving under stress. *Self-Affirmation Improves Problem-Solving under Stress*, 8(5). doi: 10.1371/journal.pone.0062593.

De Bellis, M. D., & Zisk, A. (2014). The biological effects of childhood trauma. *Child and Adolescent Psychiatric Clinics of North America*, 23(2), 185-222. doi:10.1016/j.chc.2014.01.002.

Dell, M. (n.d.). *Tap Yourself Free*. Retrieved February 24, 2018, from http://www.tapping.com/e-book.html.

Duignan, B. (n.d.). *What's the difference between a psychopath and a sociopath? And how do both differ from narcissists?* Retrieved December 21, 2019, from https://www.britannica.com/story/whats-the-difference-between-a-psychopath-and-a-sociopath-and-how-do-both-differ-from-narcissists.

Eddy, W. A. (2018). 5 Types of people who can ruin your life: Identifying and dealing with narcissists, sociopaths, and other high-conflict personalities. New York: TarcherPerigee.

Eisenberger, N. I., Lieberman, M. D., & Williams, K. D. (2004). *Does rejection hurt? An fMRI study of social exclusion*. PsycEXTRA Dataset. doi: 10.1037/e633912013-635.

Few LR, Miller JD, Rothbaum AO, et al. Examination of the Section III DSM-5 diagnostic system for personality disorders in an outpatient clinical sample. *J Abnorm Psychol.* 2013;122(4):1057–1069. doi:10.1037/a0034878.

Firtel, R. (2019, July 5). The danger of trauma bonds - know the signs. Retrieved December 28, 2019, from https://robynfirtel.com/trauma-bonds-in-a-relationship/.

Ford, J. D. (2017, August 15). Treatment implications of altered affect regulation and information processing following child maltreatment. Retrieved September 18, 2019, from https://www.healio.com/psychiatry/journals/psycann/2005-5-35-5/{d828c6b2-d67b-4ec1-b1f5-de2ba399c9f4}/treatment-implications-of-altered-affect-regulation-and-information-processing-following-child-maltreatment.

Franco, F. (2018, March 19). *Attachment and C-PTSD: How complex trauma gets in the way*. Retrieved July 28, 2019, from https://www.goodtherapy.org/blog/attachment-and-c-ptsd-how-complex-trauma-gets-in-the-way-0322185.

Gattuso, R. (2018, March 28). Complex PTSD: How a new diagnosis differs from standard PTSD. Retrieved December 20, 2019, from https://www.talkspace.com/blog/complex-ptsd-versus-standard-ptsd/.

Goleman, D. (2010). *Emotional intelligence*. London: Bloomsbury.

Greenberg, E. (2016). Borderline, narcissistic, and schizoid adaptations: The pursuit of love, admiration, and safety. New York, NY: Greenbrooke Press.

Hammond, C. (2018, November 10). *The Narcissistic Cycle of Abuse*. Retrieved November 10, 2019, from https://pro.psychcentral.com/exhausted-woman/2015/05/the-narcissistic-cycle-of-abuse/.

Hammond, C. (2019, June 29). What is narcissism awareness grief (NAG)? Retrieved August 2, 2019, from https://pro.psychcentral.com/exhausted-woman/2018/07/what-is-narissism-awareness-grief-nag/.

Hartney, E. (2019, May 12). Do You Know About Dissociation? Retrieved August 5, 2019, from https://www.verywellmind.com/what-is-dissociation-22201.

Hodges, S. D., & Myers, Michael W. (2007). Empathy. In R. F. Baumeister and K. D. Vohs (Eds.), *Encyclopedia of social psychology* (pp. 296-298). Thousand Oaks, CA: Sage.

Hoermann, Ph.D., S., Zupanick, Psy.D., C., & Dombeck, Ph.D., M. (2019). *Problems with the Diagnostic System for Personality Disorders*. Retrieved Jan 26, 2019, from https://www.mentalhelp.net/articles/problems-with-the-diagnostic-system-for-personality-disorders/.

Kluger, J. (2011, October 27). *Narcissists know they're obnoxious, but love themselves all the same.* Retrieved July 10, 2019, from http://healthland. time.com/2011/10/27/narcissists-know-theyre-obnoxious-but-love-themselves-anyway/.

Kohut, Heinz (1968). The Psychoanalytic Treatment of Narcissistic Personality Disorders: Outline of a Systematic Approach. *The Psychoanalytic Study of the Child.* London, England: Taylor&Francis. 23:86113. doi:10.1080/00797308.1968.11822951. PMID 5759031.

Kolassa, I.T., & Elbert, T. (2007). Structural and functional neuroplasticity in relation to traumatic stress. *Current Directions in Psychological Science*, 16, 321-325.

Krause-Utz, A., Frost, R., Winter, D., & Elzinga, B. M. (2017). Dissociation and Alterations in Brain Function and Structure: Implications for Borderline Personality Disorder. *Current Psychiatry Reports*, 19(1). doi: 10.1007/s11920-017-0757-y

Krizan, Z., & Herlache, A. D. (2018). The narcissism spectrum model: A synthetic view of narcissistic personality. *Personality and Social Psychology Review*, 22(1), 3-31. doi:10.1177/1088868316685018.

Lambie, J., & Lindberg, A. (2016). The role of maternal emotional validation and invalidation on children's emotional awareness. *Merrill-Palmer Quarterly*, 62(2), 129-157. doi:10.13110/merrpalmquar1982. 62.2.0129

Lamia, M. C. (2012, October 31). *Feeling is believing.* Retrieved October 19, 2019, from https://www.psychologytoday.com/us/blog/intense-emotions-and-strong-feelings/201210/feeling-is-believing

Lanius, R.A., Vermetten, E., Loewenstein, R. J., Brand, B., Schmahl, C., Bremner, J. D., & Spiegel, D. (2010). Emotion modulation in PTSD: Clinical and neurobiological evidence for a dissociative subtype.

American Journal of Psychiatry, 167(6), 640–647. doi:10.1176/appi.ajp.
2009.09081168)

Lawson, Thomas T. (2008). *Carl Jung, Darwin of the mind*. London: Karnac. p. 161. ISBN 9781849406420. OCLC 727944810.

Leary, M. (2019, May 13). What Is the Ego, and Why Is It So Involved in My Life? Retrieved December 13, 2019, from https://www.psychologytoday.com/us/blog/toward-less-egoic-world/201905/what-is-the-ego-and-why-is-it-so-involved-in-my-life

Main, M., & Solomon, J. (1986). Discovery of an insecure-disorganized/disoriented attachment pattern. In T. B. Brazelton & M. W. Yogman (Eds.), *Affective development in infancy* (p. 95–124). Ablex Publishing.

Mayo Clinic (2019) *Cognitive behavioral therapy*. Retrieved October 14, 2019, from https://www.mayoclinic.org/tests-procedures/cognitive-behavioral-therapy/about/pac-20384610

McBride, K. (2013). Will I ever be good enough?: Healing the daughters of narcissistic mothers. New York: Atria Paperback.

McBride, K. (2018, February 19). *The real effect of narcissistic parenting on children*. Retrieved October 3, 2019, from https://www.psychologytoday.com/us/blog/the-legacy-distorted-love/201802/the-real-effect-narcissistic-parenting-children.

McClelland, D., & Gilyard, C. (2008). *Calming trauma - How understanding the brain can help*. Retrieved September 18, 2019, from https://www.phoenix-society.org/resources/entry/calming-trauma-how-understanding-the-brain-can-help.

Milstead, K. (2018, October 24). *8 Types of narcissists- Including one to stay away from at all costs*. Retrieved from https://mindcology.com/narcissist/8-types-narcissists-including-one-stay-away-costs/.

Neal, B. (2017, June 25). *The science behind why people lie*. Retrieved January 19, 2019, from https://www.bustle.com/p/the-science-behind-why-people-lie-is-actually-pretty-surprising-63631

Newman, S. (2018, July 8). *3 Reasons you can't win with a narcissist*. Retrieved September 12, 2019, from https://psychcentral.com/blog/3-reasons-you-cant-win-with-a-narcissist/

Ni, P. (2018). *Understanding narcissism's destructive impact on relationships—an indispensable reader*. Retrieved from https://nipreston.com/new/project/understanding-narcissisms-destructive-impact-on-relationships-an-indispensable-reader/.

NPD Statistics. (2019, September 21). Retrieved September 21, 2019, from https://www.therecoveryvillage.com/mental-health/narcissistic-personality-disorder/related/npd-statistics/#gref.

O'Donohue, William (2007). *Personality Disorders: Toward the DSM-V*. Thousand Oaks,California: SAGEPublications. p. 235. ISBN 9781412904223. Archived from the original on 8 September 2017.

Oldham, J. M. (2015, June). The alternative DSM-5 model for personality disorders. Retrieved from https://www.ncbi.nlm.nih.gov/pmc/articles/PMC4471981/.

Paris, Joel (April 2014). Modernity and Narcissistic Personality Disorder. *Personality Disorders: Theory, Research, and Treatment*. Washington, D.C.: American Psychological Association. **5** (2): 220–226. doi:10.1037/a0028580. PMID 22800179.

Phillips, J. (2015, September 25). PTSD in DSM-5: Understanding the changes. Retrieved August 30, 2019, from https://www.psychiatrictimes.com/ptsd/ptsd-dsm-5-understanding-changes.

Pune Mirror | Updated: Jul 2, 2019. (n.d.). *Is the 'silent treatment' killing your relationship?* Retrieved November 17, 2019, from https://punemirror.indiatimes.com/others/you/is-the-silent-treatment-killing-your-relationship/articleshow/70029879.cms.

Ronningstam EF, Maltsberger JT. Part X: Personality Disorders. *Gabbard GO. Gabbard's Treatments of Psychiatric Disorders.* Fourth Edition. Washington DC: American Psychiatric Publishing; 2007. Chapter 52: Narcissistic Personality Disorder, pages 791-804.

Saeed, K. (2019, August 5). *How to deal with the silent treatment and gain the upper hand.* Retrieved December22, 2019, from https://kimsaeed.com/2019/07/28/how-to-deal-with-the-silent-treatment-and-gain-the-upper-hand/.

Schwartz, A. (2019, December 17). *Complex PTSD and attachment trauma.* Retrieved July 20, 2019, from https://drarielleschwartz.com/complex-ptsd-and-attachment-trauma-dr-arielle-schwartz/#.XgqDVUdKhPY.

Sederer, Lloyd I. (2009). *Blueprints Psychiatry* (Fifth ed.). Philadelphia: Wolters Kluwer/Lippincott Williams & Wilkins. p. 29. ISBN 9780781782531. Archived from the original on 11 January 2017 – via Google Books.

Skodol, A. E., Bender, D. S., & Morey, L. C. (2014). Narcissistic personality disorder in DSM-5. Personality Disorders: Theory, *Research, and Treatment*, 5(4), 422–427. doi: 10.1037/per0000023

Skylar. (2018, November 19). The Gray Rock Method of Dealing With Psychopaths. Retrieved January 22, 2019, from https://180rule.com/about-180rule-com/skylar/

Snowden, Ruth (2006). Teach yourself Freud. McGraw-Hill. pp. 105–107. ISBN 978-0-07-147274-6.

Stines, S. (2015). *What is Trauma Bonding?* Retrieved on December 17, 2019, from https://pro.psychcentral.com/recovery-expert/2015/10/what-is-trauma-bonding/.

Stines, S. (2018, June 5). *When you grow up as the invisible child (the impact of being raised by a narcissist).* Retrieved June 6, 2019, from https://pro.psychcentral.com/recovery-expert/2018/06/when-you-grow-up-as-the-invisible-child/.

Stines, S. (2019, July 8). *Narcissist's Mixed Messages.* Retrieved June 15, 2019, from https://pro.psychcentral.com/recovery-expert/2019/04/narcissists-mixed-messages/.

Vaknin, S. (2008, November 21). *The Dual Role of the False Self.* Retrieved on 2019, July 24 from https://www.healthyplace.com/personality-disorders/malignant-self-love/dual-role-of-the-false-self.

Vaknin, S. (2008, November 27). *The Inverted Narcissist.* Retrieved on 2019, October 25 from https://www.healthyplace.com/personality-disorders/malignant-self-love/the-inverted-narcissist.

Vaknin, S. (2008, November 30). *Narcissists, narcissistic supply and sources of supply.* Retrieved on 2019, October 29 from https://www.healthyplace.com/personality-disorders/malignant-self-love/narcissists-narcissistic-supply-and-sources-of-supply

Walker, L. E. (2017). *The battered woman syndrome.* New York: Springer Publishing Company.

Weinheimer, J., Russo, J., Giblock, D., & Kuber, J. (2020, January 27). *NPD statistics.* Retrieved January 30, 2020, from https://www.

therecoveryvillage.com/mental-health/narcissistic-personality-disorder/related/npd-statistics

Wingenfeld, K., & Wolf, O. T. (2014). *Stress, memory, and the hippocampus.* Retrieved November 12, 2018, from https://www.ncbi.nlm.nih.gov/pubmed/24777135

Zweig, Connie (1991). *Meeting the Shadow.* Los Angeles: J.P. Tarcher. ISBN 0-87477-618-X. p. 24.

Bibliography

3 Steps to identifying a narcissist. (n.d.). Retrieved from https://www.psychologytoday.com/us/blog/5-types-people-who-can-ruin-your-life/201808/3-steps-identifying-narcissist.

Dodgson, L. (2018, May 27). *How to spot a covert narcissist*. Retrieved July 19, 2019, from https://www.businessinsider.com/how-to-spot-a-covert-narcissist-2018-5.

Ford, J. D. (2005). Treatment implications of altered affect regulation and information processing following child maltreatment. *Psychiatric Annals*, 35(5), 410-419. doi:10.3928/00485713-20050501-07.

Peterson, S. (2018, June 11). *Effects*. Retrieved Jan 24, 2019, from https://www.nctsn.org/what-is-child-trauma/trauma-types/complex-trauma/effects

Schneider, A. (2015, March 25). *Idealize, devalue, discard: the dizzying cycle of narcissism*. Retrieved July 23, 2019, from https://www.goodtherapy.org/blog/idealize-devalue-discard-the-dizzying-cycle-of-narcissism-0325154.

Streep, P. (2017). *How narcissistic parents scapegoat their children*. Retrieved July 26, 2019, from https://www.psychologytoday.com/us/blog/tech-support/201711/how-narcissistic-parents-scapegoat-their-children.

Tips, R., & Children, P. (2019). *Psychologists confirm narcissistic parents are incapable of loving their children*. Retrieved Jan 24, 2019, from https://

iheartintelligence.com/narcissistic-parents-incapable-of-loving-their-children/.

Toll, A. (2013). *Be honest with me: an exploration of lies in relationships.* Retrieved Jan 10, 2019, from https://dc.uwm.edu/cgi/viewcontent.cgi?article=1168&context=et.

Enhance Your Experience

To get the best experience possible with this book, get the "Lemon Mom's Companion Workbook: Action Steps to Understand and Survive Maternal Narcissism" available on Amazon.com and wherever books are sold.

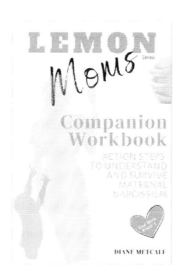

Acknowledgments

The last few years have afforded me the time and inclination to write this book. I have discovered that writing a book is a surreal practice! Transforming an idea into a written format is as complicated as it sounds, and the experience was both challenging and rewarding. I especially want to thank those whose efforts and encouragement helped bring this legacy of healing into existence.

To my husband, Kim, a simple "thank you" doesn't begin to reveal the depth of gratitude I feel for you. Our deep and relevant conversations along the way were both inspiring and affirming. Your limitless patience and belief in me were my safe haven. You kept me going when I felt like quitting. You are my rock, and I love you. I hope you're ready for the next one!

I'm forever indebted to my daughter, Christin Daurelio, for her keen insight, encouragement, and advice. You positively impacted my thoughts and helped me stay in a good emotional space. Thank you for your open-mindedness, honesty, and willingness to be involved.

I'm eternally grateful to my son, Matthew Duhé, for his encouragement, ideas, and support. Your awareness, instincts, and discernment were always welcome bonuses. Thank you for the generous gifts of your time and expertise in remastering the audio files for the upcoming audiobook.

I'm deeply appreciative of my sister-in-law Mel Harrington and my friends Val Catallozzi and Gayle Shinder, three brilliant women who generously donated their time to proofread, edit, and provide constructive criticism. They questioned the nuances of the script and pressed me to clarify and explore certain concepts. You three made the difference.

To my friend of five decades, Kim Mizell, thank you for always being the person I could turn to during those dark and desperate years. You sustained me with your friendship, compassion, acceptance, and understanding. I'm forever grateful to you.

To proof-readers, Grace Godfrey, Sharon Spencer, and Debbie Blades, thank-you for your constructive criticism. Your honest feedback was invaluable and made the book that much better!

To my mentor, and fellow author, Lise Cartwright, thank you for the hours of conversation, laughs, and coaching. Your extensive knowledge and experience were truly instrumental. I couldn't have written or published this work without you!

To my designer Christos Angelidakis, and my formatter, Debbie Lum, thank you both for your perfectionism. The book looks great inside and out. You guys rock!

To Katie Chambers, my ever-patient editor at Beacon Point, thank you for being my wordsmith. You made my thoughts, ideas, and words resonate with clarity.

To my book club peeps, Karen Anderson, Diane Askwyth, Val Catallozzi, Cheryl Gainsford, Sheila Gillis, Audrey Sauer, and Gail Shinder, thank you for continuing to ignite the spark of my imagination and my love for reading.

To my immediate and extended family, I love and appreciate each of you more than you know. Your existence makes my world a happier place.

And to my mother, thank you for bringing me into the world. Without you, I wouldn't be the person I am today.

About the Author

Diane is an experienced advocate, speaker, and writer on abuse and family dysfunction. As a result of her own healing journey and continued personal growth, she developed strong coping skills and strategies. She happily shares these with others who want to learn and grow in their own recovery. Diane holds a Bachelor of Arts degree in Psychology and a Master of Science in Information Technology. She has worked in numerous human service fields, including domestic violence, abuse, eldercare, and developmental disabilities.

She is the author of the highly praised "Lemon Moms" series. This emotionally supportive collection explains maternal narcissistic traits and teaches how to reconcile past hurts, begin healing, and move forward. Currently, Diane writes about recovering from hurtful relationships by using healthy strategies and recovery tools on her blog, "The Toolbox" (toolbox.dianemetcalf.com.) She currently lives in Nevada with her husband and adorable pets.

This book is intended for informational purposes only and is not a substitute for professional therapy.

What's Next?

When you go from unsupportive inner dialogue to affirming who you are as your authentic self, you can literally change your self-identity.

Lemon Moms Life-Altering Affirmations, Change Your Self-talk, Change YourSELF

and

I AM: A Guided Journey to Your Authentic Self, Full Color Workbook and Journal

How to write the highest vibrating, most powerful affirmations to manifest love, positivity, peace, self-confidence, motivation, success, and other wonderful things

Available on Amazon and wherever books are sold.

Love this book?
Don't forget to leave a review!

Every review matters a lot!

Your review helps others find the book, and it helps make future versions better!

Head over to Amazon (or wherever you purchased this book) to let me know your thoughts.

Thank you very much. I appreciate you!

Author Site: **DianeMetcalf.com**

Get FREE SHIPPING on books!

Made in the USA
Monee, IL
27 April 2023

f20302d6-f550-4c32-8860-7da467159888R01